Endorsements

"My friend Sam Poe's work on Biblical Storying has been of enormous benefit to me in my ministry serving churches in many nations. It has radically changed my approach to teaching, preaching and training. The study guide "Share The Story" is an essential and powerful tool to enable us all to teach the whole counsel of God to the majority of oral learners in the nations of the world."

-David Devenish, team leader Newfrontiers Together Team and Catalyst Network of Churches.

"As a Bible Storying consultant and trainer, I am often called on to review training resources. When Sam asked me to review the 'Share the Story' Study Guide, I was pleasantly surprised to see the nice balance of simplicity for those new to Biblical Storying and thorough coverage of all the essential and key considerations for a successful, productive, and purposeful sharing of Bible stories. The lessons have a nice balance between the methodology needed by missionaries and Westerners and yet a gentle reminder of the need for worldview awareness for others. Don't be misled by the simplicity as the lessons are thorough and do-able by anyone desiring to become an effective biblical storyteller. This training resource joins others that have been developed for a variety of users and needs. For me, several places in the lessons left me thinking: 'Why didn't I think of that?' I think users will agree."

- J. O. Terry, Bible Storying author, consultant, and trainer

"As a church that takes seriously the command to make disciples, both locally and globally, we have searched for a resource that would give us an effective strategy. It needed to be biblical, highly reproducible, and cross-cultural. It needed to result in followers of Jesus who not only knew the story they were in, but who entered the story and lived it. With one broad strategic stroke that could play out in a myriad of specific ways, we wanted disciples made, leaders trained and churches planted.

'Share the Story' is that resource. Sam Poe has been living the story for decades now, teaching and applying this strategy all over the world. This study guide is a gift to the church."

- Ian Ashby, lead pastor of New Frontiers Church Portsmouth, NH, USA and regional leader for Newfrontiers USA churches in the Northeast.

"Before Sam and Marlene Poe shared the biblical storytelling strategy with us, we had never heard of people as oral learners. We had to apply it straight away. This approach gave us answers to the many questions we had as leaders trying to make disciples of Jesus.

Once we understood the main principles of biblical storytelling, we were eager to learn and to change both our attitude and actions in teaching our people the Word of God. I have heard many positive reports from people using this method in a variety of different contexts, such as the Sunday service, Bible or Missionary training, leadership meetings, and home groups.

I'm quite certain if we are serious about fulfilling God's Commission to go and make disciples, we have to do it in Jesus' way, and that way is Storytelling. He is our Great Teacher and

He set the best example for us to follow. Sam's training course on Bible Storytelling is boundlessly helpful and practical. It transformed my methods of teaching and preaching."

- Valeriy and Narina Kudaev
Valeriy, elder at Armavir Church of Jesus Christ in South of Russia and regional leader for family of evangelical churches in the North Caucasus. Narina, his wife, is the principal of an award winning school in Armavir.

SHARE THE STORY: A STUDY GUIDE

Copyright © 2017 Samuel Poe.

New Frontiers Church, Portsmouth, USA.

Unless otherwise stated, Scripture quotations are taken from The Holy Bible, English Standard Version® (ESV®), copyright © 2001 by Crossway, a publishing ministry of Good News Publishers. Used by permission. All rights reserved.

TABLE OF CONTENTS

Page

2	Endorsements
6	Foreword
8	Acknowledgement
9	Introduction
11	Sample Course Structures
12	SESSION 1: We Have a Story to Tell
17	SESSION 2: Fulfilling the Great Commission
21	SESSION 3: Overcoming Cultural Barriers to the Gospel
27	SESSION 4: The Whole Counsel of God
31	SESSION 5: Selecting and Telling Stories to Reach a Culture
36	SESSION 6: Called to Make Disciples
42	SESSION 7: A Strategy for Starting New Churches
47	SESSION 8: Where Do We Begin?
51	SESSION 9: Preparing to Tell the Story, Part 1
57	SESSION 10: Preparing to Tell the Story, Part 2
63	SESSION 11: Helping People Engage with the Story
70	SESSION 12: Practical Activity
71	Appendix A: Orality and Literacy Worldwide
72	Appendix B: The Value of Biblical Storying in Post-Modern Culture
75	Appendix C: The Story of Redemption
76	Appendix D: Exercise in Story Selection with a Focus on Worldview Issues
78	Appendix E: Leading Discussion with Head-Heart-Hand Questions
79	Appendix F: Selected Recommended Reading

Foreword

My experience with the Share the Story strategy began in the mid 1980s when Marlene, our children, and I moved to Mexico to share the good news about Jesus. While preparing for cross-cultural living, I learned about storytelling as an invaluable way to share the gospel in a cross-cultural context. I made it my goal to learn to tell the story of my life and of coming to faith in Jesus in Spanish, as well as to develop the ability to share key stories from the Bible to help our new friends in Mexico understand God's big story of salvation. I became increasingly convinced that story-telling as a way to share the good news cross-culturally was vital because people can receive a story-teller much more readily than a foreigner whom they perceive as trying to impose new religious ideas upon them. And because the world is growing increasingly cross-cultural in cities and towns, the need to share the gospel effectively with people of other cultures without even moving to other countries is quickly becoming the task of the majority of Jesus' followers, not just a few select missionaries.

While in Mexico, I met Terry Virgo, the founder of the Newfrontiers family of churches, which began in England in the 1970s. Over the next years in Mexico we met a number of people related to Newfrontiers, and through those relationships we -- and the church we had planted there -- became a part of this movement.

After ten years, the Lord prompted us to move back to the USA in order to connect with Terry and the work he was doing at that time helping some churches become part of Newfrontiers. Later, David Devenish, one of the key leaders in Newfrontiers, invited me to be a part of a task team, comprised of different leaders from various nations, that would gather regularly for a season to develop strategies for sharing the gospel with people of other nations. Knowing something of my background in storytelling, David asked me to get further training in Biblical Storying in order to help our movement develop this strategy to reach out to the unreached peoples of the world. So I took a crash course in Chronological Bible Storying led by J.O. Terry at the Southwestern Baptist Theological Seminary in Fort Worth, Texas, whereupon many new horizons regarding the value of Biblical Storying opened up.

The Importance of knowing God's big story

Many today have virtually no knowledge of the story of the Bible. By going through the major stories of Scripture from Genesis to Revelation that reveal God's great salvation plan through his Son, Jesus Christ, we are helping them to see their need for the salvation that only Jesus can bring them. For those who have already become followers of Jesus, these same stories can lead us on in life together with Him as our leader and King. As we hear these stories, engage with them through discussion, and enter into their life together, we are changed. We begin to see life more through the lenses of a biblical worldview, and the fact of one's literacy or lack of it is not a primary factor. Everyone has opportunity to hear, engage, and live the story in genuine community. This approach can easily become the springboard for seeing new churches started.

A Reproducible Strategy

The storytelling strategy is also highly reproducible in many different contexts. It is a relational activity among people everywhere in the world. Friends always tell each other stories. As people come into relationship with Jesus and his followers and practice telling and engaging in biblical stories through discussion, they are encouraged to enter into the life of that story together in community. With that, they can picture themselves doing the same thing with their family and friends. Those more mature in their faith can help encourage and equip them for this task. Since this strategy is very flexible, it can serve in all kinds of community situations, from one-on-one to larger group interaction. Reproducibility is one of Biblical Storytelling's most vital features.

These are some of the primary reasons we have prepared this study guide for Share the Story. It is intentionally cross-cultural, it imparts a biblical worldview, and it is highly reproducible. I trust this training will be of help to you and your friends as you set out to make known the story of Christ's salvation. It is the most wonderful story human ears will ever hear!

Sam Poe

Acknowledgements

There are so many people that have been a part of my journey into Biblical Storying. I thank the Lord Jesus for bringing each one of them into my life and for giving me the privilege of walking with them along the varied paths this journey has taken in various nations of the world.

I would like to particularly acknowledge the training and advice I have received from J. O. Terry. His input has been very valuable in putting together the material for the "Share the Story" video training and this study guide.

I want to express my appreciation for Abigail McFarthing who worked many hours helping to formulate the training questions and activities throughout the guide.

Also, a big thanks to Lissie Cooley, Sue Zelie and Gareth Forsey for the editing they did on this book.

Finally I want to thank my dear wife, Marlene, who has been my constant companion every step of the way along this journey that now stretches across decades. Her continual willingness to reach out to others and serve them in love has been a powerful influence in my life and a real expression of God's grace among those with whom we have had the privilege of sharing God's great salvation story. She truly lives "The Story."

INTRODUCTION

The Vision

The gospel we have been commissioned to share with the world is the story that the Bible tells. It starts in Genesis and ends in Revelation. It is important that every church acquires a means of telling essential aspects of God's great salvation story for all those who are coming into the life of the church. They should have the opportunity to hear key redemptive stories shared in chronological order to better understand the grand narrative of the Bible. Selecting and telling key stories from the Bible is an essential part of the process. This training has been designed to lead you through that process.

In addition to going chronologically through key redemptive biblical stories, biblical storytelling certainly can have many other expressions. They may include telling a cluster of stories from Scripture around a special theme or need within the group, focusing on a particular book of the Bible, or exploring the life of a particular Bible character such as Abraham or King David. There is a great deal of flexibility within the "Share the Story" strategy.

This study guide presents "Share the Story" as a unified strategy. You will learn how to use Biblical Storying as a way to share the gospel, make disciples, train leaders, and plant churches. Its effectiveness in these regards has been field-tested. Storying's best credential is that Jesus himself modeled it, as did the early Christians who carried on his mission in the book of Acts.

Hear the Story

As human beings we are wired for stories. The process of telling and hearing stories lies at the heart of every friendship. We are shaped by the stories we hear. All community life is built on commonly held stories. Jesus, the Son of God, continually told stories to catch his hearers up into the wonderful community that he had known throughout eternity with his Father and the Holy Spirit, one Living God in three magnificent Persons. Hearing these stories from the Bible is an essential part of entering this eternal fellowship Jesus came to draw us into.

When we hear individual stories from the Bible in the context of the big story from Genesis to Revelation we begin to see more clearly our identity, destiny and meaning in the light of the grand narrative of the Scriptures. Even the non-narrative parts of the Bible (like poetry, prophecy and letters) truly make sense when they are understood within God's big story,

Engage the Story

As we explore together the stories that we hear, discussing questions that arise as a result, we begin to discover the truth that the stories proclaim. Good storytelling typically leads toward discussion. Rather than trying to explain what the story means, it is generally most effective to ask key questions that enable the group to engage with the story from God's Word. Learning to serve the group in the discussion process is an important part of this training course.

As we engage with the stories together we start to see how our own individual stories connect to God's story. This engagement with the Bible story makes a way for us to engage in one another's lives as we seek to follow Jesus together as our Savior and King.

Live the Story

Stories lend themselves to action. We live our lives as stories, not as well-organized bullet points. Stories can be messy, just like our lives. Grappling with the biblical story, and trying to hear what God is teaching us through it, helps us apply it to our lives in a much more concrete way. As we engage with the stories and allow them to shape our hearts and actions, we find ourselves entering the life that they proclaim. Life transformation occurs in this environment. We find we are being drawn into God's plan to have a people who live in loving relationship with him and who reach out to bless those around them. Together in community, as we receive the power of the Holy Spirit promised to us, we begin to truly live out God's story in our world today. In such a loving, safe, non-threatening environment there should be regular opportunities given for prayer and the exercise of spiritual gifts to bring healing, help and encouragement to each one as they seek to live the story in their own life. New strength and enablement can come to share the story of God's salvation through his Son, Jesus, everywhere we go, so that many might know eternal life in him.

How to Use the Study Guide

To get the most benefit from this study guide, you should **watch each training video** before you complete the corresponding session in the study guide. You can watch the videos on the internet by registering online at biblicalstorying.com. You can also order the DVDs by writing to info@biblicalstorying.com . However, if you do not have access to the online videos or the DVDs, this study guide can stand alone as a resource to train you in Biblical Storying.

We designed this study guide so that you can **complete it in a group**. As you discuss the questions with others and practice telling stories and leading discussion, you will gain the understanding and skills necessary to use Biblical Storying effectively. Of course, if you are not able to be in a group, you can still use this study guide individually.

Regardless of whether or not you are able to watch the videos or be part of a group study, we encourage you to **write down your answers** to the questions in a notebook so that you can engage the material more fully.

Timing and Schedules

We envision this study guide being used in a twelve- to thirteen-week course, but you can structure your training in the way that best fits your needs. Please also note that while every session contains questions and activities to help you engage the material, Sessions 8-12 include a special ongoing assignment that will take you through the practical steps of preparing, telling, and leading discussion on a Bible story.

On the next page we have included a couple of ideas for ways that you could structure the course. Keep in mind that each video runs between 30-60 minutes, and we anticipate that reading the study guide and completing the questions on your own will also take you 30-60 minutes. Finally, we recommend leaving 30-60 minutes for the group discussion and activity at the end of each session.

Sample Course Structures for Use with the Study Guide

If you plan to watch the videos together as a group:
- 13 weeks of group meetings
- Each meeting = about 2 hours
- Time to complete work at home = 30-60 minutes

If you plan to watch the videos individually at home:
- 12 weeks of group meetings
- Each meeting = about 1 hour
- Time to complete work at home = 1-2 hours

Meeting	Introduce course. Watch Video #12 (example storying session)
At home	No homework
Meeting	Watch Video #1, Group discussion/activity for Session #1
At home	Read Study Guide Session #1 and complete questions
Meeting	Review answers for Study Guide Session #1. Watch Video #2, Group discussion/activity for Session #2
At home	Read Study Guide Session #2 and complete questions
Meeting	Review answers for Study Guide Session #2. Watch Video #3, Group discussion/activity for Session #3
...continue this pattern...	
Meeting	Review answers for Study Guide Session #10. Watch Video #11, Group discussion/activity for Session #11
At home	Read Study Guide Session #11 and complete questions. Practice story for final meeting
Meeting	Watch Video #13 (example storying session). Group mock storying final activity!

At home	Watch Video #12 (example storying session) & Video #1. Read Study Guide Session #1 and complete questions
Meeting	Review answers for Study Guide Session #1. Group discussion/activity for Session #1
At home	Watch Video #2. Read Study Guide Session #2 and complete questions
Meeting	Review answers for Study Guide Session #2. Group discussion/activity for Session #2
At home	Watch Video #3. Read Study Guide Session #3 and complete questions
...continue this pattern...	
At home	Watch Video #11. Read Study Guide Session #11 and complete questions
Meeting	Review answers for Study Guide Session #11. Group discussion/activity for Session #11
At home	Watch Video #13. Practice story for final meeting
Meeting	Group mock storying final activity!

If you plan to complete the course on your own:
- Allow about 12 weeks
- 2 hours of work per week, depending on if you are able to watch the videos or not

SESSION 1: We Have a Story to Tell

> *If you have access to the videos, you will find it helpful to watch Video #12 first, a model storytelling and discussion session of the story of Cain and Abel. This will give you an idea of what storying looks like in action.*
>
> *The following material is based on Video #1. If you have access to the videos, you can watch this session in advance, and then complete the study guide below.*

I. What is Biblical Storying?

Biblical Storying represents a paradigm shift towards an oral, communal approach to Bible teaching. What does Biblical Storying look like in action? One person tells a story from the Bible to a group, and then leads the group in a discussion of the story, helping them engage with the story so they can apply it to their lives personally or as a group. Individual stories can be grouped in several ways. They can be clustered around a theme; they can be used to address particular needs of a people-group; or, of perhaps greatest benefit, they can be told chronologically over time, giving the listeners an over-arching picture of the Bible's Big Story.

II. Why Use a Chronological Approach to Bible Storying?

A. The Bible is a story

The Bible is essentially the story of how God has acted in history to bring glory to his name, reconciling us and the world we live in back to himself in the face of the tragic consequences of sin and death. Through what Jesus has accomplished by his death, burial, resurrection and ascension, he made the way for all who trust in him to enjoy a full reconciliation and relationship with God. This story reveals Jesus as the King of kings and Lord of lords. Those from every nation and culture who put their trust in him as risen and eternal King are made partakers of his life and become participants with him in his great salvation story. They will ultimately dwell with him in a renewed universe, in complete and untarnished joy forever. And all this is to the praise of his glory!

God is not only the author of this story, he is also the story's primary character. Many people have a tendency to view the individual stories of the Bible as different illustrations of moral principles that we should all try to live by. However, as we begin to comprehend the big story of the Bible, we come to understand more clearly that God has given us this story to reveal who he is, what he has done, and the glorious splendor of his kingdom.

Some may argue that though the Bible is indeed made up of narrative sections, it is also comprised of many other types of writing, including poetry and wisdom literature, prophetic writings and epistles full of instruction and teaching. This is true, but every part of scripture is a part of the big story being told, and it is ultimately not possible to fully understand these various parts without seeing how each fits into that wider story.

For example, many of the poems and songs found in the book of Psalms would be difficult to grasp fully without the context of the stories they so often refer to.

📖   Read Psalm 105.

☞   What are we instructed to "make known" and "tell of" (v.1-2)?

☞   Through the rest of the psalm, what stories does the author refer to as reasons for our praise?

It's clear that the psalmist assumes we will be familiar with the stories he draws upon. More than that, he strongly urges that these stories be told to everyone from every nation. This same direction applies to much of what the prophets of scripture spoke, and to what is written in the epistles. We are to tell the story.

B. Many individual stories make up God's Big Story

God's work in specific times and places, with specific individuals or groups of people here in this world, discloses his overall plan. Without the knowledge of these individual stories, it is not possible to see the grand panorama of his undertaking-- but at the same time, we need to know the Big Story arc to make sense of each individual story.

Even long-standing church members can tend to think of the Bible as simply a sort of library of isolated stories. For example, on one occasion they hear a message about King David, at another time one about the Apostle Paul, and then later on something from the life of Jesus. Certain points or moral lessons are drawn from each story, but the hearer may not really understand that each of these stories is just a portion of a much bigger story. As a result, they fail to catch the beauty and value of each of these in their context. This kind of 'cherry-picking' can lead to serious misunderstanding about the message of the whole Bible.

☞   Can you think of some individual Bible stories that might be misunderstood without the context of the overall Big Salvation Story?

Once the smaller stories are understood in the bigger context, their impact goes beyond the control of our own piecemeal selections, and we can begin to see our own small stories as part of God's bigger story, too.

C. Many people lack knowledge of God's Big Story

We must not assume that people generally know the Big Story of the Bible. There are many-- even Christians, and even in cultures where Christianity has had a presence for years-- who have no basic understanding of the entire biblical story. As followers of Jesus, we must give attention to telling God's Big Salvation Story in an understandable and interesting way.

If those with whom we want to share Christ's offer of salvation don't hear the Big Story, they will be left with many gaps in their understanding of what Jesus has accomplished for us through his death and resurrection. They must hear key individual stories from the books of Genesis

> Once a young couple began to attend meetings at our church. We decided to invite them over on a Sunday afternoon to have lunch and talk about their interest in our church. As we chatted that afternoon, they shared that they were thinking that it would be good to be part of a church now that they had begun a family so that their children could grow up with a moral foundation in their lives. When we asked if they had any questions about our church, they quickly answered, "We really don't know anything about church or the Bible. We think you are going to have to tell us some stories."
>
> They were insightful. They realized that in our culture many attend a church to get some moral foundation. They knew they had very little experience with what that would mean. But they were sure that there was a story that they should hear that would undergird that foundation. They were totally correct. There is a Big Story for them to hear.

to Revelation in order to understand that the God of the Bible is the Creator of all things, that he reigns as King over all nations and his kingdom is eternal, and that he has made covenant promises and he keeps the promises he has made. Without exposure to the worldview brought to us by the story of the whole Bible, the grave danger lurks of perceiving particular truths of the Gospel in the light of old cultural mindsets, and wrong worldview assumptions may remain unchallenged.

D. Jesus used this model

A strong reason to use a chronological approach is that it follows the model demonstrated by Jesus. Jesus gives us a powerful example of the importance of starting at the beginning of the story and going through to the end during his walk with the two disciples on the Emmaus Road.

📖　　Read Luke 24:13-35

When Jesus joins the disciples, they don't recognize him. The two are sorrowful and confused about what had just happened in their lives. Everything seems in shambles. Now, here is the newly resurrected Jesus walking along with them. He wants to show them who he actually is. Given that, you might expect him to perform some amazing sign to show them that he has risen from the dead. But he doesn't.

☞　　What does Jesus do instead?

☞　　What does this show us about how Jesus viewed the Bible?

☞　　In Luke 24:27, Jesus shows the disciples (and us) the focus of God's Big Salvation Story. What is it?

☞　　In Luke 24:32, what is the disciples' reaction to hearing the Big Story?

E. Jesus is the Master Storyteller

Not only was the Big Story important to Jesus, but during his ministry here on earth he also placed great value on telling individual stories.

☞　　Matthew 13:34 describes how Jesus spoke to the crowds. What did he use to teach them?

The stories he told were not simply illustrations to make a point; they *were* the point. For example, Jesus' parables were carefully crafted. They:
- engaged the attention of the listeners
- evoked a response from them
- were particularly memorable for retelling
- were intriguing, even for people who did not like the point of the story
- used the language and daily experience of the common folk
- forced people to grapple with truth and try to understand it for themselves
- revealed realities of the kingdom of God to those whose hearts were open
- challenged those with closed hearts to examine their own wrong thinking and skepticism
- encouraged people to keep coming back to hear another story, opening up a possibility that their hearts would finally open to the truth

We can follow Jesus' example, telling stories that are memorable, intriguing, and relevant-- and allowing the truth to penetrate people's hearts and worldviews.

III. Why "Share the Story"?

"Share the Story" is a strategy for sharing the gospel, making disciples, and planting churches through telling God's Big Story from the Bible. This is not a new strategy. As we tell these stories we are following the example of Jesus, the Master Storyteller.

It's important for every church to develop a plan to share God's great salvation story that begins in Genesis and carries through to Revelation, for all those who are being added to the church family. They should get the opportunity to hear key redemptive stories from God's Word and participate in discussion around each story. During these times, questions may arise indicating that the story has challenged concepts in the hearers that run counter to the truth of God's Word. This will help those involved in the training process to recognize where extra focus is needed. Additional related stories can be chosen to help the group more clearly understand the things they find challenging.

In addition to this sharing the grand narrative of the biblical story from start to finish, biblical story-telling can have many other expressions. They may include telling a cluster of stories from Scripture around a special theme or need within the group. Going through a book of the Bible step-by-step, telling key stories from that book, can be of great value. For example, going through a Gospel (or the Gospels) on the life of Jesus is vital to our journey together as his disciples. A series of stories from the Book of Acts is important in order to capture an understanding of God's plan for the church. Exploring the life of a biblical character such as Joseph, Ruth or Daniel, could be very helpful in addressing issues of Christian growth and maturity in the group. Clearly, there is a great deal of flexibility within the "Share the Story" strategy.

Questions for Discussion:

1. Do you think most of the people where you live and work have an understanding of God's Big Salvation Story?

2. Why do you think Jesus so often used stories when he taught? List as many reasons as you can think of.

3. If you could choose ten stories from the Bible that would tell God's Big Salvation Story, what stories would you choose? (You can discuss this question as a whole group, or work in smaller groups and then share your group's ideas with everyone.)

Activity:

Break into groups of two or three. Choose one of the passages below (if there are multiple groups, the leader should try to ensure that each group chooses a different passage).

- Romans 4
- Galatians 4:21-31

- 1 Timothy 1:12-17
- 2 Timothy 3:10-12
- Hebrews 7
- Psalm 8
- Psalm 51
- Psalm 77

Next, work together in your group to find the background stories that your chosen passage refers to. Finally, share your findings with the whole group: briefly tell the background stories, read the text, and then explain how the stories help you understand better the meaning of the text you have chosen (and how the text may shed light on the stories!).

SESSION 2: Fulfilling the Great Commission

The following material is based on Video #2; if you have access to the videos, you can watch this session in advance, and then complete the study guide below.

I. The Great Commission

📖   Read Matthew 28:18-20

Jesus' last words to his disciples define our mission as Christians. It's important, then, that we know what that mission includes.

☞   What do you think Jesus meant when he said "all nations"? (For a hint, read Revelation 7:9)

This is a big mission! We need an effective way to reach cultures and worldviews that are totally different from our own. The strategy of storying can help us fulfill Jesus' command to make disciples of all nations.

II. The Story of the 72: Jesus' Methods of Evangelism

Let's look at a story from the Bible to learn some principles of how to reach people with the good news about Jesus. While on earth, Jesus spent time with his disciples preparing them to participate in his mission. At times he sent them out to towns and villages to do what he had been doing and to tell the stories about his kingdom that he had been telling.

📖   Read Luke 10:1-11, 17-21

Let's think about the instructions Jesus gave the 72.

A. Where were they to go?

Literally, the disciples went into the local towns and villages.

Symbolically, however, it is likely that Jesus chose the number 72 because Jews of that time considered there to be 72 nations that made up, or represented, all the peoples of the world.

Later, in the Great Commission, Jesus made it perfectly clear that he was sending us to all the nations (people-groups) of the earth.

> Seventy-two nations are mentioned in the Greek version of the Old Testament in Genesis 10. You might notice that some translations of Luke speak of Jesus only sending 70 disciples-- why the discrepancy? Because 70 corresponds with the number of nations mentioned in the *Hebrew* version of Genesis 10. Either way, Jesus was making a point that his followers are to think globally in their mission.

B. How were they to go? (verses 1-3)

First, he sent them in teams of two.

☞ Can you think of other times that Jesus did things in the context of team? Why do you think he valued teams so much?

Next, they were to pray to God for workers. They had to depend on God; they could not make disciples on their own. Finally, in terms of method, they had to trust God for his help and protection of them personally.

☞ In what ways would the disciples have to depend on God as they went?

C. What were they to bring? (verse 4)

☞ What did Jesus tell the disciples to bring with them?

They were not to be hindered by bulky or burdensome material. Similarly, if you go to a place that is hostile toward the gospel of Jesus, you may not be able to bring extra Christian resources. You can, however, go with the stories of the Bible in your heart and mind. Unhindered by loads of printed materials that may put you at risk and weigh you down, you will just go as Jesus instructed.

D. How would they be provided for? (verses 5-8)

☞ Who would give the disciples food and lodging?

Jesus instructed the disciples to stay with people and eat with people. As they went, God would meet their needs through the people they would befriend. Jesus also shows us the importance of food! As we go to other cultures (or even to your own), eating the food of that people is a vital step in building relationships. If you won't eat with them, how can you become friends with them? Over a meal, we can naturally talk and share stories.

E. How were they to make the Good News known? (verse 9)

☞ What two things did Jesus tell the disciples to do in each place they went?

> When we lived in Mexico, I prayed for a woman who was sick, and God healed her. She then wanted me to go talk to many of her friends about Jesus and pray for them as well. Her job was teaching proper etiquette to people who lived and worked among the upper class. As a result, I was able to share the Gospel with people whom I otherwise never would have met.

When supernatural power and compassion accompany the gospel, who knows what the repercussions may be? Because Jesus gives his disciples authority to do his works of healing and deliverance in his name (Luke 9:1), they get to demonstrate and then proclaim his gracious kingdom.

☞ How would you explain "the kingdom of God" to someone who is not yet a Christian?

Telling people that the kingdom of God has come near them will require telling some stories. God's Big Salvation Story underlies an understanding of the kingdom of God. People must hear what the prophets foretold: that the Liberator King, the Son of David, would come. And when Jesus did come, he constantly told stories, especially parables to depict what his kingdom was like.

☞ How did Jesus explain the kingdom of God (also called the kingdom of heaven)? (see Matthew 13:24-33, 44-50)

Storytelling avoids all sorts of problems associated with sharing the gospel in another culture.
- Because everyone enjoys a good story, the teller more easily crosses any cultural boundaries.
- Because it is the story that brings the teaching, rather than a person from another culture, there is no opportunity for any sense of cross-cultural superiority or inferiority.
- It does not matter if the listeners are unable to read. Everyone can hear the story and interact with it.

About two-thirds of the world's population are oral learners; that is, they rely on spoken rather than written language for communication and learning. Of this group, some have no ability to read and write. Others, however, may technically be able to read but in actual daily life rely on oral communication in order to learn new things. The tendency in many to revert back to functional illiteracy is well known among literacy workers. Even in the supposedly literate West, about half of adults function primarily as oral learners. *(See Appendix A: Orality and Literacy Worldwide)*

In contrast, it is estimated that about 90% of all gospel preaching done worldwide assumes that the hearers are literate learners. This literate style of teaching, through outlines, bullet points, and lists of principles or steps in a process, makes it very difficult for those who are oral learners to understand and remember, even when these things are presented orally. Such people learn best through hearing stories, proverbs, and word pictures-- which was Jesus' primary way of teaching.

> I remember having an oral learner share with me how difficult it was for him to grasp teachings that are based in a literate style of learning. He said, "When you start out with point one, I try to remember that. Then you come to point two and I try to remember both points one and two. Then when you come finally to point three I usually realize that I now have forgotten point one! I also feel like I'm getting a headache, so I just give up and quit trying to remember what you're saying."

F. What kind of people were they to seek? (verse 6)

☞ What kind of person did Jesus tell his disciples to look for?

As we seek to introduce people to Jesus, we too should look for individuals or families whose hearts are open to us and the stories we tell.

J.O. Terry, an expert in Bible storying, tells this anecdote:[1]

> [I remember] one day when a visitor to the library where I was visiting came to ask if I would come to his district of India and meet some of the local people. When I agreed, he then immediately set about making local contacts and arranging meetings and hospitality. One of the first was a well-respected coffee estate owner who was a member of a local community service club. Perhaps to test me, he invited me as a guest speaker at his service club meeting. I accepted. His only question to me was, "You are not going to embarrass me, are you?" I assured him I would not, though I did find a way to get in an appropriate illustration from the Bible.
>
> Later, team members and I got to share with him and his family in his home and to pray for God's blessing on his family. One must be sensitive with people of peace as they are probably going out on a limb to connect you to their friends. One of my overzealous colleagues nearly destroyed the relationship in this particular instance by demanding a salvation decision this dear man was not yet ready to make.
>
> Through this initial person of peace who was not even of that tribal group, I was able to visit some 80 families among the tea and coffee plantation owners in that district and be warmly welcomed by all who in turn opened other doors to their relatives and their estate workers, giving us a reason for a presence in their area. And it all started with a story.

God gave J.O. a man of peace, and though he himself was not yet a Christian, he helped open many doors for sharing the gospel story.

From Jesus' method of sending out the 72, we have seen some principles for how we should spread the gospel. We also saw, implied in both the sending of the 72 and the Great Commission, the need for telling stories in order to communicate the good news of God's kingdom more effectively to "all nations."

Questions for Discussion:

1. Has the Lord ever led you to a person of peace who has opened doors for you to share the good news about Jesus with others?

2. Do you feel Bible storying is important to fulfilling the Great Commission? Why? Why not?

3. What are some ways that you could use Bible storying in sharing the gospel?

Activity:

In groups of two or three, pick a story from the Bible that you feel demonstrates the kingdom of God (NOT one of Jesus' parables that is specifically about the kingdom). Explain to the whole group why you chose that story, and what aspect of the kingdom of God it exemplifies.

---

[1] Terry, J. O. "Bible Storying in the Worthy Home with the Person of Peace and the Family of Peace." p. 14.

SESSION 3: Overcoming Cultural Barriers to the Gospel

> *The following material is based on Video #3; if you have access to the videos, you can watch this session in advance, and then complete the study guide below.*

I. Culture Affects Understanding of the Gospel

In the 1970s a missionary started a church in a tribal group. Due to health problems, he and his family had to leave the work after only a short time. Another missionary was assigned to go and complete the work that the first missionary had begun.

Soon the incoming missionary began to discover that though the people carefully followed the forms of "having church" which they had picked up from the previous missionary, they had not understood the real gospel message. Therefore, they were treating the Christian God like they treated the evil spirits whom they feared from their own cultural background. They were faithfully carrying out the rituals of "church" that they thought were necessary so that the "Christian God" would leave them alone!

When the incoming missionary tried to bring corrective teaching to this situation, he found it fruitless. The people had no real sense of what it meant to have a relationship with God, and therefore no real interest in knowing more about him.

Finally the missionary realized that they needed a basic exposure to who God is and what he is like. To grasp that, they had to see the big picture of God's salvation plan from the beginning in Genesis before they arrived at the story of Jesus and the cross. He began teaching through key Old Testament stories in chronological order. Before he had finished, the people were already coming under conviction of sin and had begun to realize their need for a savior. When they heard of what Jesus has done for us through his death, burial and resurrection, they were ready to respond to the Good News!

Until these people truly began to understand God's Big Salvation Story from start to finish, they tended to treat the message about the Christian God, which had been given through piecemeal corrective teachings, in much the same way that they treated the demon gods they feared within their own cultural and religious understanding. Their main goal was to do the necessary rituals to placate the gods and try to keep them off their backs.

As they came to understand something of God's big redemptive story that begins in Genesis and carries through to Revelation, they began to long to know this wonderful Savior King who had come into the world to make a way for them to once again be in relationship with the all-powerful and loving God of the Bible who had created them in His own image. They could find their supreme joy in walking with Him.

☞ Can you think of any misunderstandings about the gospel that might arise in people of your own culture if they were to hear teachings about Christianity "piecemeal" as did the people in this story?

II. Worldview: The Roots of Culture

Everyone has a culture that he or she belongs to. Culture can be defined as an integrated system of patterns of behavior, feelings, values, and beliefs that are determined by the commonly held worldview of that society. Actions done in accordance with one's culture are usually done at a subconscious level-- they grow out of the hidden "roots" of one's worldview.

To better understand culture, we can think about it in terms of a tree:

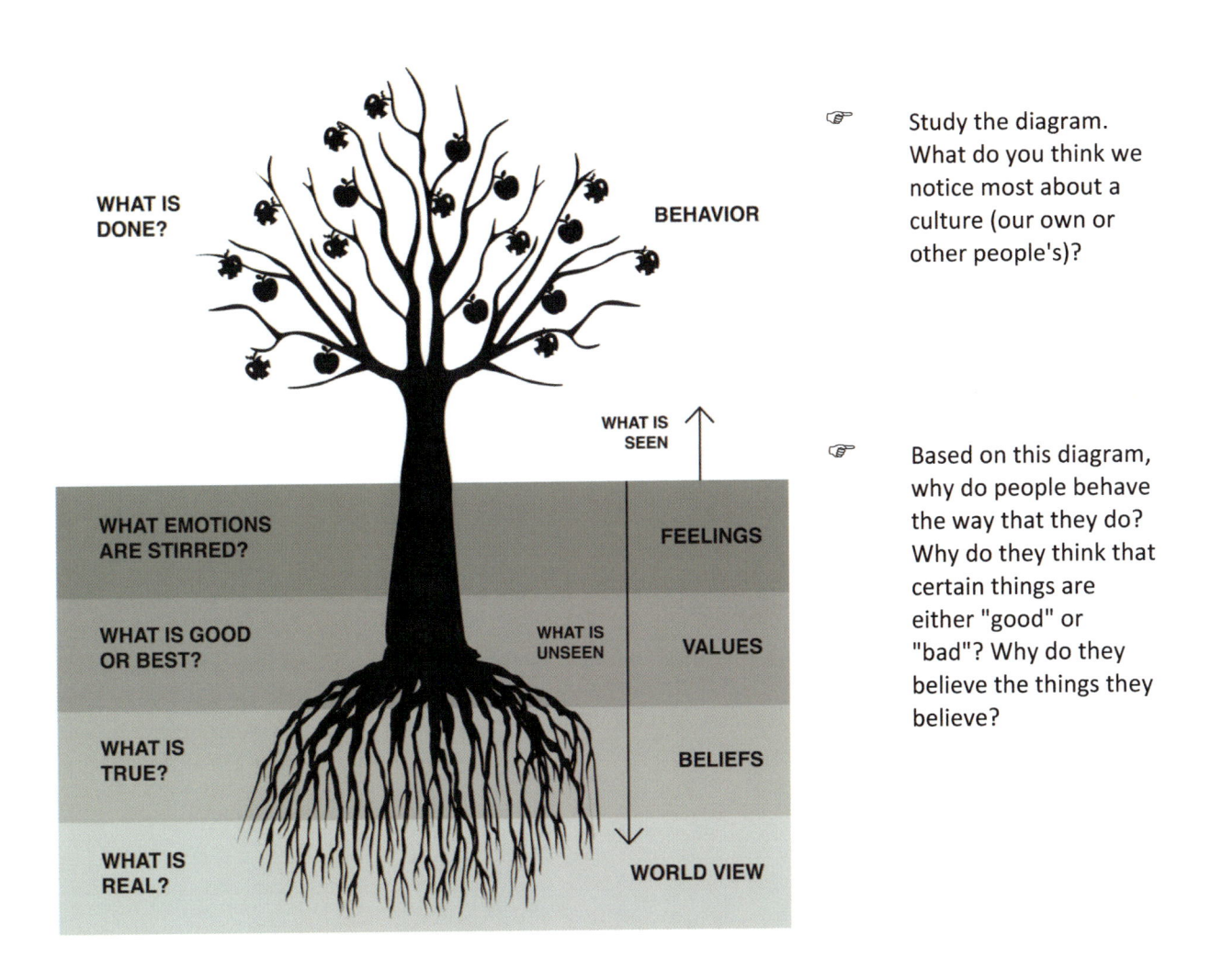

☞ Study the diagram. What do you think we notice most about a culture (our own or other people's)?

☞ Based on this diagram, why do people behave the way that they do? Why do they think that certain things are either "good" or "bad"? Why do they believe the things they believe?

When we first encounter a culture different from our own, we tend to notice people's external behavior-- the "fruit" of their cultural tree (and we usually tend to focus on the negative aspects of the culture, the "rotten fruit," although, of course, cultures also have positive elements too!). Merely addressing the negative behavior, however, is useless because behavior is driven by a culture's deeper feelings, values, and beliefs, which in turn are shaped by the prevailing worldview.

Hidden beneath the surface, a society's worldview forms the "roots" of its culture. Worldview deals with the deepest assumptions about life: Who are we? Where did we come from? Where are we going? What is the nature of the world we live in? Why is there evil and suffering and finally death? What happens to you after you die? The answers that people give to these basic questions affect their beliefs, values, and feelings, which in turn determine their outward behavior-- the "fruit."

Trying to make external behavioral changes in a people-group without a worldview change will not make true disciples of Jesus. The best it can produce is externalism (keeping the rules) and ritualism (going through the right forms and rituals). This is true in every nation of the world.

If worldview is so essential in determining a people-group's beliefs, values, feelings and actions, we need a way to effectively discern, engage, challenge, and alter people's worldview assumptions when they create a barrier to receiving the gospel.

III. Analyzing Worldview and Its Effects

In the secular Western culture that I grew up in, there are many worldview assumptions that lie beneath the attitudes and practices within that culture. (See Appendix B: The Value of Biblical Storying in Post-Modern Culture)

An example of an underlying assumption would be the commonly held materialist worldview that believes the physical universe is all that there is-- there is no spiritual realm, and therefore no involvement from a supernatural Creator. This worldview gives rise to a belief in the narrative of evolution apart from any direction by God: everything, including life, is driven by random events, mutations, and the survival of the fittest. Belief in this story shapes society's values: the greatest "good" is that people get whatever they feel will make them happy right now. This makes it reasonable to think that striving to get whatever one desires in order to fulfil this appetite is what life is all about. This has given rise to the consumeristic life style so common in our culture that has an insatiable desire for "more". This has led to the careless wastage of natural resources and the exploitation of the world's poor and most vulnerable in an effort get all the goods desired at the least cost to the consumer.

> A missionary who had been working with a tribal group in the jungles of Central America was going to take the chief of the tribe up in his airplane. Before leaving, the chief gathered some of the key men of the tribe together and sucked on each of their mouths. The missionary had never seen this done before so he later asked the chief why he had done this. The chief explained that he had learned this from the missionary himself. He had taken note that the missionary would gather each of his family members together before going somewhere in the plane and "suck on each of their mouths." The chief understood that this was powerful magic to be used when going up in the plane to ensure a safe journey. Two worldviews had produced two very different interpretations of the same external behavior![2]

The first stories of the Bible clearly reveal that the whole creation is good and made to bring glory to God. Humankind was created to live in loving relationship with God and be his appointed stewards to care for the earth (Genesis 1-2). This biblical worldview leads to a very different life-style.

☞ Choose one of the following behaviors (or think of one) to analyze:
- A business-person habitually stays late at work, to the detriment of his or her family.
- A mom desperately tries to make her house spotlessly clean before guests come over.
- A teenager changes her personality and dress style when she arrives at a new school.
- Your friends are living together, and they say that they're not interested in getting married. What are the underlying worldview assumptions, beliefs, values, and feelings that could lead to this behaviour.

IV. Stories Challenge and Change Wrong Worldview Assumptions

---

[2] Hiebert, Paul G. (1981). "Finding a Place and Serving Movements Within Society." In Ralph D. Winter & Steven C. Hawthorne (Eds.), *Perspectives On The World Christian Movement* (p. 368). Pasadena, CA : William Carey Library

Since worldviews are so foundational, we must think carefully about how people form their worldviews, and how we can help change their worldviews to line up with the biblical worldview. A person's worldview is not based on abstract propositions or lines of logic. It is essentially based in a narrative-- a big story-- regarding what is real.

A. Overcoming barriers to the gospel

We will find it very difficult to argue someone out of a worldview assumption. In order to overcome a wrong worldview, we need to replace the underlying narrative with a new story. Jesus taught through stories. He intended his stories to challenge existing worldview assumptions and to provide an alternate picture of the reality that he called "the kingdom of God."

> "[I]t would be quite clearly wrong to see [Jesus'] stories as mere illustrations of truths that could be articulated in purer, more abstract forms. They were ways of breaking open the worldview of Jesus' hearers, so that it could be remoulded into the worldview which he, Jesus, was commending" (N. T. Wright. [1992]. *The New Testament and the People of God*, Minneapolis, MN: Fortress Press. p. 77).
>
> "[S]tories are actually peculiarly good at modifying or subverting other stories and their worldviews. Where head-on attack would certainly fail, the parable hides the wisdom of the serpent behind the innocence of the dove, gaining entrance and favour which can then be used to change assumptions which the hearer would otherwise keep hidden away for safety" (ibid, p. 40).

📖 Read the parable of the Workers in the Vineyard (Matthew 20:1-16) or the parable of The Pharisee and Tax Collector (Luke 18:9-14).

☞ How would the story you read have challenged the hidden assumptions of Jesus' listeners? What aspect of the "kingdom worldview" was Jesus trying to communicate through this story?

Stories are like anchors for any given perspective on the world. When that perspective holds people away from knowing the joy of being in relationship with Jesus, the best thing a Christian can do in order to displace that perspective is to tell better stories. And we do have better stories! Our stories provide answers to the essential questions of life.

☞ Think back to the behavior you chose to analyze in the previous section. What story could you tell from the Bible that might challenge the worldview underlying this behavior? For example, to challenge the worldview underlying the practice of abortion, you might choose the story of Creation (that people are made in the image of God) or of John the Baptist (called by God and responding to the Holy Spirit even before he was born!).

B. Connecting with bridges to the gospel

Because of God's gracious working among people everywhere in spite of their sin and brokenness, cultures not only have worldview barriers to the gospel, but they also have worldview bridges that can help people to connect with the gospel story. We should look for those bridges and capitalize on them!

For example, in my own Western culture, that is now heavily influenced by post-modern thought, places a high value on equality, tolerance, and social justice *(see Appendix B: The Value of Biblical Storying in Post-Modern Culture)*. Biblical stories that highlight aspects of these themes can provide bridges for the gospel and touch the hearts of those living within this culture. Examples of such stories might be the story of Ruth or the Good Samaritan.

☞ Once again, think about the behavior you have been analyzing. You have identified the underlying worldview and chosen a story that could challenge that worldview's barriers to the gospel. Now, choose a story from the Bible that might connect as a bridge with someone who holds this worldview:

We'll be looking more at worldview barriers and bridges in Session 5.

The more biblical stories people know and can connect into the big story of God's saving work, the more completely they are able to embrace a biblical worldview. This change of their fundamental view of the world will influence a wide array of beliefs and practices that grow out of that core and hold them in darkness. Remember, the Holy Spirit is at work through the telling of the biblical story.

As we encourage people to discuss the stories, they gain greater opportunity to discover how the story applies to their life and world. The Holy Spirit will reveal personal applications to the hearts of those who listen. Taking time to discuss the story together often enhances that process.

During these discussion times, those who are sharing the story must remain alert to pick up on any of the hearers' misunderstandings of the story. We may need to retell the story and lead further discussion for clarification. We may recognize worldview issues that are holding the hearers away from truly responding in faith to Christ's salvation. With this understanding we will be better informed in choosing other stories that will continue to address these issues.

Questions for Discussion:

1. Can you think of any worldview assumptions in your culture that form barriers to people responding to the gospel? (You may want to read about post-modern culture in Appendix B)

2. What stories from the Bible could you tell to confront those worldview assumptions?

3. Can you think of any positive worldview assumptions in your culture that could form natural bridges for the gospel?

4. What stories from the Bible could you tell to connect with these worldview assumptions?

Activity:

Which of the stories you discussed above would fit well as part of a basic set of stories for sharing the gospel among the people you are connecting with?

SESSION 4: The Whole Counsel of God

The following material is based on Video #4; if you have access to the videos, you can watch this session in advance, and then complete the study guide below.

I. "The Whole Counsel of God" Through the Bible

The apostle Paul was on his way to Jerusalem, knowing he would probably be arrested there. Facing the prospect of prison and death, he met the elders from the church in Ephesus and gave them a farewell speech. What would Paul say to them, as he looked back on his time of ministry in Ephesus?

📖 Read Acts 20:17-38

☞ Why does Paul claim that he is "innocent of the blood of all"?

Paul's sweeping statement raises the question: How did he know he had declared the "whole counsel of God" to the church under his leadership? Did he teach through every single verse in the Bible (the Old Testament)? How could he be sure that he had completed the task of preaching everything that needed to be preached?

A. The Old Testament

Paul would have been familiar with this phrase from Old Testament scripture.

📖 Psalm 33:6-11 mentions "the counsel of the Lord":
"By the word of the LORD the heavens were made, and by the breath of his mouth all their host. He gathers the waters of the sea as a heap; he puts the deeps in storehouses. Let all the earth fear the LORD; let all the inhabitants of the world stand in awe of him! For he spoke, and it came to be; he commanded, and it stood firm. The LORD brings the counsel of the nations to nothing; he frustrates the plans of the peoples. The counsel of the LORD stands forever, the plans of his heart to all generations."

☞ What biblical events does this passage describe as examples of the "counsel of the Lord"?

We see that understanding of the whole counsel of God begins by knowing his big redemptive story, starting with the creation of the universe.

B. Jesus' example

Not only did the apostle Paul have the Old Testament example of seeing "the whole counsel of God" as a big story, but he had Jesus' example as well. We have already looked at how, on the day he rose from the dead, Jesus went through this big story with the two disciples on the road to Emmaus. He showed those disciples how all of God's Big Salvation Story in the Bible is consummated in himself.

C. The early Christians

Jesus' followers in the Book of Acts followed this same approach. For example, Stephen on the day he was martyred preached his final sermon as a story.

📖 Read Acts 7

☞ What Bible events and characters did Stephen include in his sermon?

The hearers became enraged as Stephen reached the climax of his story and sermon: Jesus, the Righteous One, had been betrayed and murdered by some of the same men listening to Stephen that day. As they stoned him, Stephen followed in the footsteps of Jesus and prayed, "Lord, do not hold this sin against them" and saw Jesus himself receiving him into eternal glory.

In another example of how the early Christians used this concept of the "whole counsel of God" in declaring the gospel, Paul preached in Pisidian Antioch.

📖 Read Acts 13:13-41

☞ What Bible events and characters did Paul include in his sermon?

Notice how Stephen and Paul chose different Bible stories, but both of them communicated something important and relevant about Jesus to their different audiences.

D. The "whole counsel of God" and us

In each of these examples, the preaching goes through the Big Story in a chronological way, unfolding redemptive truth through the whole Bible. This is the way God has chosen to make known his great salvation plan for us.

This approach is valuable for a number of reasons. For those who do not read, it is much easier to retain the stories in their memory when they are linked chronologically with other stories. Each story becomes an episode in a larger story. This also helps keep the stories from fading or changing because they are each harmoniously connected to the larger story.

Once a person gets the basic understanding of God's Big Story from the Bible, when a new story is introduced, he just needs to be told where the story fits in the Big Story and it then becomes a new episode of the story he already holds in his heart. People find it much easier to assimilate, grasp, and remember new information when it connects with their pre-existing knowledge.

II. Our Experience in Zimbabwe

We (Sam and Marlene) worked with a team in Zimbabwe to prepare a set of key stories that would paint the big picture of God's great redemptive plan-- beginning in Genesis, continuing through the life of Jesus, and going on to the outpouring of the Holy Spirit in the Book of Acts. We chose the second coming of Jesus as the final story in this set. We also chose certain stories for this set that would deal particularly with certain worldview issues that can hinder Gospel response within Zimbabwean culture. We picked 34 stories altogether, ones that would bring these particular hearers through to an initial or better understanding of the gospel.

Then we went on to select a set of stories from the book of Acts, in order to show that God plans to use his people, the church, to bless all the nations. These stories could be used as foundational for forming a new church. In a situation where there was already a church gathered, these stories helped establish the church in true biblical understanding of how God desires to work through his people by his Spirit.

Another set of stories we have worked on focuses on how Jesus trained the twelve, and what it means to be a disciple of Jesus. These stories could help people grow in their own relationship with God, and in learning how to mentor others; our goal is to make disciples who make disciples.

This process of choosing appropriate, relevant stories should happen in each place and culture where we desire to introduce people to God's Big Salvation Story. *Share the Story* is not a "one-size-fits-all" strategy. We do not alter the individual stories, but we do consider the worldview issues within that particular culture in our story selection.

Lesslie Newbigin writes, "The dogma, the thing given for our acceptance in faith, is not a set of timeless propositions: it is a story. Moreover, it is a story which is not yet finished, a story in which we are still awaiting the end when all becomes clear."[3] The Story we tell is not finished. Attentive hearers -- whose worldviews have been remodeled by the Big Story -- will find that they are one of its characters and will, by faith, step into it.

Questions for Discussion:

1. Think about the Epistles, the book of Revelation, and other non-narrative biblical material. How could you incorporate some of this material in a storying setting?

2. Choose a few of the following Psalms: Psalms 8, 16, 20, 30, 33, 57, 67. Think of particular stories from the Bible that you could pair with them in order to assist a group in worshiping God.

Activity:

In groups of two or three, choose an aspect of Jesus/the gospel (i.e., Jesus' kingly authority, substitutionary atonement, good news to the poor, etc.). Now imagine that you are giving a sermon like Stephen or Paul. Make a list of stories (both Old and New Testament) that you could use to lead up to and reinforce this truth about Jesus and the gospel.

---

[3] Newbigin, L. (1989). *The Gospel in a Pluralist Society*. Grand Rapids, MI: Eerdmans. p. 12.

SESSION 5: Selecting and Telling Stories to Reach a Culture

I. Which Stories Should We Tell?

A. Focus on key stories

The following material is based on Video #5; if you have access to the videos, you can watch this session in advance, and then complete the study guide below.

The Bible is a big book, composed of around 500 narratives. All of these stories make up parts of the Big Story. However, it is not feasible to consider telling all these stories in order to bring our hearers through to knowledge of the gospel message. Yet, as we learned in the last session, we are called to declare "the whole counsel of God." Therefore, we have to ask ourselves what the key stories are that can bring people to an adequate understanding of

- God's salvation through Christ
- what it means to become part of the family of God
- how to live as disciples of Jesus

☞ In Session 1, you discussed what ten key stories you would choose that communicate the essential message of God's Big Story. Perhaps your ideas have changed or solidified since then. What ten key stories do you think *must* be included in a story set in order to be faithful to "the whole counsel of God"? Why would you include each story? (The first one has been done as an example below. If you get stuck, you can find more ideas in "Appendix C: The Story of Redemption.")

○ *The creation of the universe shows God's power, and that all he does is good.*

B. Consider worldview barriers

A secondary aspect is important to consider when developing a set of stories to tell to a particular group of people. This has to do with worldview issues that are contrary to the gospel within that culture.

As previously mentioned, the only way to subvert these wrong worldview suppositions is to tell better stories than the current stories they believe. It therefore becomes important, especially for those entering into a new cultural situation, to recognize these "cultural strongholds" and tell better stories from the Bible than the stories that produce these strongholds within that culture.

When we were beginning to prepare our first set of stories in Zimbabwe we formulated a set of questions to ask the local people, questions which addressed their worldview issues *(See Appendix D: Exercise in Story Selection)*. A few examples of these questions include "Where did the world come from?", "What is the most important thing in your life?", and "Is there a spirit world?"

We also went to a Bible School library in Zimbabwe to find any worldview research that had been done by others on the local culture and worldview; there, too, we found very helpful information. Out of this research we discovered what worldview issues tend to hold people back from fully responding to the gospel message. For example, many Zimbabweans fear displeasing their dead ancestors. As a result, we were able to choose a number of stories from the Bible that addressed this and other worldview strongholds *(See Appendix C for the list of stories we chose for telling in Zimbabwe).*

In the process of telling the stories and leading discussion around the stories, we will often discover other wrong worldview assumptions. As storytellers it is very important to listen carefully to the questions and comments that arise in the group during the discussion time in order to detect these assumptions.

☞   Imagine that you are entering a new culture (or you want to find out more about your own culture), so you decide to make a survey and go around asking people questions in order to find out what their worldview assumptions are. What questions would you ask in your survey?

C. Recognize worldview bridges

As we consider which stories to tell, we also need to recognize bridges in the culture's worldview that can help the hearers connect with the stories. You have already done some thinking about this in Session 3. Don Richardson gives a powerful example of finding a cultural bridge in bringing the gospel to a people group.

Don and his family went to the Sawi people of New Guinea in the 1960s. The Sawi were a tribe of headhunters and cannibals. As the

> During our time in Zimbabwe we interacted with many people who live in a rural, agrarian environment. They were close to the land and quickly related to the many instances in the Bible that involve cultivation and farming. In the story of the creation of the first man and woman, I often noticed their response to that story, which tells of God placing them in the garden of Eden to "work it and care for it." The Zimbabweans had a deep understanding of this because of their life as farmers and found that the story gave dignity to the work they do. As we worked for a season among these dear folks, I began to see just how agrarian many of the stories of the Bible are-- stories of sowing and reaping, battling with weeds, the great value of water, the shepherd caring for his sheep, and so forth.

missionaries told the story of Jesus' betrayal by Judas, the Sawi rejoiced in the story: Judas was their hero! It turns out that from childhood they had heard stories exalting violence and treachery. When they heard the story of Judas, they cited one their favorite proverbs, "Fatten him with friendship for an unsuspecting slaughter."

After that day Don and his wife Carol wondered how they would ever be able to get the Big Story of God's salvation across to these people. They had met with a huge barrier to the gospel. Then war broke out between this tribe and a tribe nearby, and for weeks the tribesmen fought and killed each other. Finally Don said to the leaders of the tribe, "If you don't stop fighting, we will have to leave here." The Sawi did not want this because the Richardsons had brought medical care to them, along with other things they wanted. Also, they saw having a foreign family among them as a status symbol. Some tribal leaders came to them one night and told them, "Tomorrow we will make peace!"

On the next day Don and Carol watched anxiously as the two warring tribes gathered opposite each other. Emotions were high pitched; women were crying. Finally, a young man from their tribe grabbed his only child, a small baby, and rushed toward the enemy lines. When he got there he said, "I give you my son and with him my name!" A man from the other side approached and presented his baby to their tribe in exchange. Each child that was given was referred to as the "Peace Child." As long as the Peace Child lived in the village, peace was supposed to be maintained with the Peace Child's home village.

In this cultural custom, Don Richardson found a cultural bridge that opened the door for the gospel to come to the Sawi people. As he once again told the stories of Jesus, he told them of a loving heavenly Father, who because he wanted to make peace with us who had become his enemies, crossed over to our side by sending his only Son to dwell among us. Then Don cited the words of the Prophet Isaiah: "For to us a child is born, to us a son is given; and the government shall be upon his shoulder, and his name shall be called Wonderful Counselor, Mighty God, Everlasting Father, Prince of Peace" (9:6).

Don was able to announce to the Sawi: this child is God's Peace Child-- his name is Jesus! And because Jesus died and rose from the dead, never to die again, he is God's perfect Peace Child once and for all. He brings peace between mankind and God the Father, and peace between one tribe and another. It is a peace that lasts forever for all those who trust in Jesus.

As Don shared the story of Jesus going to the cross as our Peace Child with the leaders of those tribes, one of the men who had offered his son to the other tribe said, "If Jesus was the Peace Child, it was the worst thing anyone could ever do to betray him." The room fell silent. From that time onward those Sawi people began putting their trust in Jesus.[4]

D. Other Ideas

In your own context, think about how you might create story tracks or clusters to address the needs of those you are connecting with.

- For those who have not yet put their trust in Jesus, you could put together a short track of stories focusing on the basic story of salvation.
- For new believers, you could look at the life and ministry of Jesus through the lens of discipleship (see biblicalstorying.com under the Resources tab for a model Discipleship track).
- You could choose a particular theme to cluster a group of stories around (for example, the themes of water and its value, of sowing and reaping, of marriage, etc.).
- You could draw on the lives of biblical characters in order to instruct on particular issues.
- Other tracks could focus on the book of Acts for a vision of the Spirit-filled community, or on God's heart for the nations as seen throughout the Bible, or on the end times -- the New Heavens and Earth.

☞ Which Bible character's life would you choose stories from in order to study how to trust God through suffering? How to be a good leader? How to live for God in a pagan culture?

II. How Should We Tell the Stories?

We need wisdom, not only to choose the right stories for a culture, but to decide on the best method of sharing the stories.

Some missionaries had worked for 25 years in a tribe in Africa and had seen only about 25 baptized believers as a result. That would be an average of about one new convert per year of ministry. They had tried to communicate the gospel by preaching as they had learned in Bible School. The missionaries ended up feeling that this group was quite resistant toward the gospel.

> J.O. Terry recounts how a missionary was telling the story of Jonah to a tribal group who were primarily fishermen. He was using pictures as an aid in the storytelling. When he came to the moment in the story where Jonah is thrown overboard, he held up a picture of Jonah falling into the mouth of a monstrous fish. From that moment on the buzz in the group was, "Where can we go to catch a fish like that? That would set us all up for the rest of the year!" Well, needless to say, they missed the point of the story. Sometimes pictures can backfire!

---

[4] Richardson, D. (2005). *Peace Child*. Ventura, CA: Regal Books.

Then some of the young Christians from that tribe set the stories of the gospel to musical chants, which fit their cultural style for telling important heritage stories. Almost immediately the gospel began to multiply many times over within this people group. Within a few years about a quarter of a million of their people were worshipping Jesus.

This tribe was not as resistant as the missionaries had thought. A change in the style of sharing the gospel had made all the difference. Prior to this the message had been proclaimed but not really heard. When an appropriate oral strategy was used to proclaim the gospel, it was understood and received.[5]

When telling a Bible story, the story-teller has many options of how to present the text; these are explored in more detail in Session 10.

III. "Share the Story" is a Flexible Strategy for Choosing and Telling Stories

One of the weaknesses of taking a prepared set of stories from another context and simply applying them to the culture you are in, without first considering the worldview and circumstances of the people you want to share with, is that the prepared stories and the style of storytelling may not fit the new situation. Later, when the work starts to bog down, it is easy to say, "We tried storying and it didn't work," when in fact it was the application of the method that did not work.

As we have stressed before, biblical storying is never a "one-size-fits all" program. It is a plan of action that takes into consideration the present thinking and situation of the people we desire to reach. In the long haul this pays off great dividends as we begin to train others to carry on in this mission.

As we carry on telling the stories of the Bible it may become clear that there is a common issue among the people we are sharing with that we had not previously recognized, which could be addressed by adding another story from Scripture. This is easy to do, and the next time the stories are told in the same culture this story can be included. Also, clusters of stories can be told around a particular issue. (This might best happen after the group has knowledge of the Big Story.) Every new story they hear becomes another episode in the Big Story they already hold in their minds. We just need to let them know where the story fits into the broader context.

Question for Discussion:

Think about a particular need that you face in your own culture or church (eg., "consumerism"). Imagine you are hosting a five-week biblical storying group to address that need; what episodes from the Bible would you include in a "cluster of stories" around that topic?

---

[5] Story originally published in Lausanne Occasional Paper (LOP) No. 54, "Making Disciples of Oral Learners." Issues Group No. 25, Avery Willis, Convener, Steve Evans, Co-Convener. Lausanne Committee for World Evangelization, 2004 Forum for World Evangelization, Pattya, Thailand. September 29 -October 5, 2004.

Activity:

Break into groups of two or three. Read "Appendix D: Exercise in Story Selection with a Focus on Worldview Issues" together. As a group, look for any barriers and bridges to the gospel in the statements these rural Zimbabweans made. Next, choose ten stories from the Bible you feel would help address the barriers and connect with the bridges. Finally, share your list of stories with the whole group.

SESSION 6: Called to Make Disciples

> *The following material is based on Video #6; if you have access to the videos, you can watch this session in advance, and then complete the study guide below.*

I. Jesus Intentionally Made Disciples

📖 Read John 1:35-42 and Mark 1:16-20.

☞ What did you learn about Jesus from this story?

☞ What did you notice about those first disciples of Jesus?

Jesus called a small group of men and intentionally made them disciples, those who would carry on the work he was doing. He was intentional and purposeful, calling them to follow him and promising that he would *make* them fishers of people. In turn, they had a desire to be with him and made sacrifices to follow him.

These first followers of Jesus travelled with him. As he shared life together with them, they saw the miracles he did, and he got them involved in the work he was doing. He taught them about his kingdom primarily through stories and discussed their meaning with them. Through all these means, he was making them his disciples.

Jesus' disciple-making method involved a few key ingredients:
- A relational environment
- Storytelling and discussion about the stories as part of the disciples' training
- They observed Jesus teaching and doing miraculous works
- Jesus included them in what he was doing
- Jesus sent them out to do what he had done (Mark 6:7)
- They reported back to Jesus all that they had done and taught (Mark 6:30)
- The power of the Holy Spirit working through them!

II. Recognizing Different Stages of Maturity

A. What are the stages of growth?

In order to make disciples, we must be able to recognize where people are at in their journey with the Lord. The apostle John recognized that there were people at different levels of maturity in the churches he wrote to.

📖 Read 1 John 2:9-14

☞ What stages of spiritual maturity does this passage list? What characteristics does the passage give for each stage?

As we tell stories and lead discussions, we should keep in mind these categories of people:
- Some people are not yet born of God: They are still dead in sin, "in the darkness."
- Some are those newly born of God, or young children: Their sins are forgiven; they know the Father's love. (They are also hungry and ignorant; they need spiritual milk. 1 Pet. 2:2-3)
- Some are young adults: They have overcome the evil one, they are strong, they know the Bible. (And they are able to minister to others.)
- Some are spiritual parents: They have history walking with the Lord. (And they have become intentional about reproducing other disciples.)

Biblical disciple-making is a process that begins with those not yet born of the Spirit and follows through to spiritual adulthood. It is a process that happens in the context of "family life."

SPIRITUAL FAMILY DISCIPLESHIP CYCLE:[6]

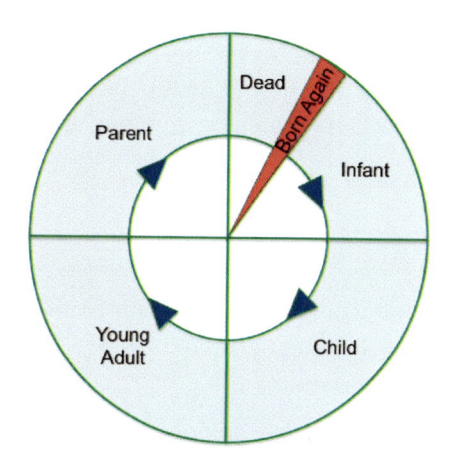

B. How can we recognize these different stages of growth?

We can discern where people are at in their spiritual growth by simply listening to what they say! A safe, relational atmosphere in which a group shares and discusses stories creates an ideal context for drawing people out and getting to know them.

Let's think about some typical responses you might hear from people in each of these stages.

- From someone not yet born of God:
  - "I think Christians are all hypocrites."
  - "I think there are many ways to God."
  - "I'm a better person than many people I know. Surely God would accept me if he exists."
    - ☞ What else might they say?

- From one newly born, a child:

---

[6] This illustration is drawn from: *Truth That Sticks: How to Communicate Velcro Truth in a Teflon World* by Avery T. Willis Jr. & Mark Snowden. Colorado Springs, CO: NavPress, 2010, p. 138

- o "I don't understand! Why? Why?"
- o "I have been very involved with witchcraft and I think it harmonizes with following Jesus."
  - ☞ What else might they say?

- From a young adult:
  - o "Bob wasn't at our small group tonight; I'll check on him to make sure he's OK."
  - o "I shared my story with a friend at work and he didn't want to receive Jesus. I must have done something wrong."
    - ☞ What else might they say?

- From a spiritual parent:
  - o "I'll take John with me the next time I go visit someone who is sick."
  - o "There are two guys in my group who I think are potential leaders. I'm going to look for opportunities to spend some extra time with them."
    - ☞ What else might they say?

C. Every member of the storying group is of equal value

As we seek to identify what stage of spiritual growth people are at, we must remember that we are not making a value judgment on them.

- Parents need children or the group will soon become a geriatrics unit with no growth.
- Children need parents or they will not mature.
- There is health and safety in such a family atmosphere.
- Everyone gets in the action. Remember, it's not a) believe b) come to maturity c) serve, but rather a) believe b) serve c) come to maturity (Ephesians 4:11-16).
- There is grace for all. Remember each of us can have a bad day and act momentarily like a baby. In this kind of transparent community there can be help and encouragement for each one.
- Discipleship is not based just on "one-on-one" relationships. It happens in community through various gifts and ministries.
- Those who are leaders (spiritual parents) facilitate this process.

III. Intentionally Helping People Mature

Once we've identified where people are at in their spiritual growth, how can we, as intentional disciple-makers, help them continue to mature?

A. For someone not yet born again

You may share aspects of your own story of coming to know God. Also, begin to share God's Big Salvation Story and talk with them about it. It is usually good to begin with some of the stories in Genesis that are so foundational to coming to know God in the light of the Bible.

As we share biblical stories in chronological order, it is important to let them respond to God in the light of the stories being told. As we come to the stories of Jesus we can give them opportunities to call on him and put their trust in him. It may be necessary to get together separately with those who are beginning to awaken to their need for Christ early on and share more quickly the stories of God's salvation through Christ's death and resurrection. If this is happening in the entire group, it may be appropriate to do a streamlined presentation of the Gospel with them all and then continue to tell the stories where you left off in more depth.

B. For someone newly born again or a spiritual child

Continue to share God's Big Story with them. Help them understand who they are "in Christ." Help them come into the Spirit-filled life. Help them understand what it means to be part of the family of God.

We should be willing to begin sharing these things with new believers as they are responding to the gospel. I would recommend being prepared to present a fast-tracked set of stories/teachings on the importance of water baptism and being filled with the Holy Spirit that can be easily shared at any point along the way as new believers are added to the group. These things could be shared with just those who are coming through to faith or in some cases with the whole group, especially if a number of them are responding together. We need the wisdom and direction of the Holy Spirit as we are helping people come through to being true disciples of Jesus. Prayer is vital at every turn.

C. For young adults in Christ

Begin training them to "Share the Story" with others. Provide ministry opportunities, coaching, and mentoring for them.

As leaders it is essential that we begin to model teamwork as soon as possible in a group of new believers. As we begin to include others in this process we are already starting to build an understanding of what being added to God's family, the church, looks like. Everyone has something to contribute. Everyone is called to serve.

D. For spiritual parents

Help them understand this reproducible model for making disciples. Include them in the process. Release them to make disciples.

It is important to say here that those who are moving into being spiritual parents may not always be those who have been Christians for many years. Those who are responding to Christ in genuine faith and commitment may grow to this stage fairly quickly. An important key to moving forward in this reproducible model is to have others coming into the function of spiritual parents as soon as possible.

"Share the Story" is a simple and reproducible strategy. Every single disciple can help make disciples.

IV. A Story from India

The story of Mangal Kishu illustrates this process of newborn Christians growing into spiritual parents-- of disciples making other disciples.

Mangal and his wife grew up in India practicing the tribal religion they were born into. Mangal had a fourth grade education and could read a little bit; his wife could not read at all. Mangal and his wife came to believe in Jesus and became part of a church. When war broke out in their area, their pastor was killed by terrorists, and Mangal and his family had to flee to a refugee camp.

A Bible storytelling training program was starting in a city eight hours away. Mangal and his wife decided to enroll for the training. After they completed it, Paul Koehler, who was leading the training, told them, "Go back to your village and wherever you go, tell these Bible stories to others." Mangal describes his experience:

> I was so happy to be telling the Bible stories. I would call the people in one place to tell them the stories, and they were listening-- our Santal people love to hear stories. Even the "Hindu" people (non-Christians) were very interested to hear the stories. At nighttime, I would gather the people in one household and tell them the Bible stories. So this is how I was telling the stories and people were listening and enjoying it.
>
> During this time I was doing day labor work in the field in Serfanguri. Many people would work together in the field squatting in lines while we cleaned the row of jute grass. It takes all day to do the work. So while we were working together, I was telling them the Bible stories and they were listening and laughing. The people there did not know the word of God, so these stories from the Bible were new to them. They would hear the stories in the field during the days, and at nighttime we would get together and learn the story-songs. They enjoyed those stories and they learned them. When we were working, wherever I would go, then this group of people would also go with me, because they liked the stories that I was telling. So while I was working I was also telling those stories, sometimes healing stories, miracle stories, so many kinds of stories.
>
> One day one family asked me, "See brother, you are telling such healing stories. We have a two year old daughter but she is not walking yet. She is like a lame person. Will you do something for us? You told us about the God in those stories. Can that God heal my daughter?" So I told them, "If you believe in this God, then your daughter will be healed." They agreed and said to me, "Yes, we will receive and worship that God."
>
> So at evening time, when I would go there and tell them stories, I prayed for that girl. She became healed and the whole family accepted Jesus Christ as their Savior. I called my supervisor and they took water baptism. Over time, two or three other families came to the Lord, so we started a fellowship there.
>
> So through these stories I have established two or three churches so far. Because of that I love these stories very much. Those stories are made by God only. They are powerful and people are hearing them and believing, and their lives are changing. Because of that, nowadays I am only telling stories, I am not telling anything else. I am only doing storytelling. Through the stories the work of God is going on and growing fast. I have won many souls. I have been teaching my believers those stories, and they are learning them. I am so happy to tell the stories. I love the stories, because stories are loved by everybody, whether animist or Christian. Nobody denies the stories. And through the stories, the word of God is very easy to share, to do the ministry and to bring the people to Christ.[7]

Questions for Discussion:

1. In one or two sentences, how would you summarize Jesus' disciple-making strategy?

---

[7] Koehler, P. F. (2010). *Telling God's Stories with Power: Biblical Storytelling in Oral Cultures.* Pasadena, CA: William Carey Library. pp.192-194.

2. In the light of Jesus' method of making disciples, how would you picture disciple-making happening in your own life? With whom?

3. What potential do you see for biblical storying as it relates to ongoing Bible teaching and training among those you are connecting with?

Activity:

In groups of two or three, think of stories from Jesus' life and ministry that give us insight into what it means to be his disciple. Which of these stories would you choose to help a new believer grow as a follower of Jesus?

SESSION 7: A Strategy for Starting New Churches

The following material is based on Video #7; if you have access to the videos, you can watch this session in advance, and then complete the study guide below.

I. The Church: God's New Community

A. The church is God's strategy

📖 Read Ephesians 2:19-22

☞ To what does the apostle Paul compare the church (the community of Christians) in these verses?

☞ What is the reason that we are "joined together" and "built together"?

The church in every place is a family, a household, and a temple assembled by Jesus and dwelt in by God's Holy Spirit. God wants each church to grow and multiply, thereby blessing cities and nations around the world.

B. Biblical storying helps build Christian community

As people become followers of Jesus, God intends that they be gathered into a community of believers, a local church. Throughout the book of Acts, disciples of Jesus made new disciples and churches were established.

Biblical storying can play a significant part in this process because storytelling helps create community.

☞ How do you think storying can help build a sense of community among a group of people?

Whenever we come together with friends, we share the stories that make up our lives. Sooner or later we begin to tell our heritage stories, the stories that have formed us and tell where we came from. For Christians the stories of the Bible are a major part of our heritage. As we share our stories of coming to faith in Jesus and the stories upon which our faith is based from the Bible, community around God's Big Salvation Story is beginning.

Have you ever noticed how hearing one story often brings to mind another story that is somehow akin to the first one? As we intentionally share stories from the Bible with others and interact around the stories, we are apt to tell our own unique stories. As we share and listen, we start to see life through one another's eyes. Our lives begin to be woven together through the life experiences we share, and we begin to see how our own life story can be woven together with God's Big Story. This is what every human heart really cries for-- to be known and understood by God and his people.

> In one small group gathering I shared the story of Cain and Abel. After I finished the story and we began discussing the story together, I asked, "Does anyone here have a story from your own life that you were reminded of as you heard this story?" One young man shared how he was so jealous of his brother that he once broke out in rage against him. Others also then admitted to having similar stories. This led us into a very powerful time of prayer ministry for each other.

Today the art of storytelling is rapidly gaining popularity throughout the world, even among more literate cultures. People have a hunger for true and meaningful relationships. Shared stories of our histories, failures, and joys are the fabric that knits us together in community. In a world where many feel isolated from real relationship, many yearn to be in an environment where they can share their struggles and defeats as well as victories and triumphs.

> ☞ Imagine you are in a small group, hearing Bible stories and then connecting them with stories from your own life. Pick two stories from the Old Testament and two from the New Testament and link them with personal stories of your own. (For example, the story of Abraham waiting for the birth of his long-promised son might lead naturally to sharing a story from your own life of how you had to wait in faith for a promise from God to be fulfilled.)

As followers of Jesus we have stories to tell, stories of our own sin and redemption. We also have our grafted-in family history, the stories of the people who knew God in the Bible. And most wonderful of all, we can share the good news that anyone who puts his trust in Jesus is made a part of God's amazing and eternal family. What better story is there to tell?

II. Building Reproducing Churches

A. The need for a reproducible strategy

In our last session, we looked at the example Jesus gave us as he trained his followers to be disciples who go out and make other disciples. This same example carries over into starting multiplying churches. In order to build churches that will multiply, we must ensure that they have a reproducible strategy instituted right at the beginning.

When we share life together and engage around stories from God's word, we are making disciples in the same way Jesus did. Through this process, we are also equipping those called to areas of leadership so that this process can continue to propagate. Then, as the small group grows, it will be able to branch into two groups, and as these small groups of believers on mission multiply, a new, reproducing church will be established in that region.

When we have told Bible stories in different places, people have shared with us that they can picture themselves doing it too. Many people find it difficult to picture themselves doing what a pastor often does on a Sunday morning, standing before his congregation and expounding point-by-point on a passage of scripture. However, when they hear someone tell a story from God's Word and participate in a discussion around that story, they can picture themselves doing that in a small group of friends.

> ☞ What advantages (or disadvantages) do you see in teaching God's Word using storying in a discussion-based, small group setting? What makes storying easy to reproduce across many small groups?

Through the reproducible, Biblical Storying approach, the gospel can be shared by many people, not just the few particularly skilled ones.

B. A real-world example

A video called *EE-TAOW*[8] tells the story of a missionary named Mark Zook. Mark's church sent him and his family to the Mouk tribe of Papua New Guinea. There they undertook learning the language and culture of the Mouk people. Once he had grasped the basics of the language and culture, Mark set out to share the gospel with these people who knew nothing of the Bible. He began teaching through the Bible chronologically, starting in Genesis and working his way through to the resurrection of Christ. The day came when Jesus' resurrection was depicted in drama form. That day nearly their whole village came to faith in Jesus. It is a wonderful story of a new church being born.

That same day Mark began to speak with the new believers about how they were to take this message of God's salvation to other villages around. Some people from a nearby village came and offered money to buy a missionary to come to their village and share the story. Of course, Mark made it clear that you cannot "buy" a missionary or "buy" the gospel; it is a gift. However, such calls as these caused Mark to come up with a reproducible strategy to start churches in the surrounding villages.

This was his plan: he would take some of the Mouk believers to the next village. There Mark would teach through the Bible stories and the Mouk believers would help by participating in aspects of the teaching. In the third village Mark asked the Mouk believers to do the teaching and he would help. When the people in the village complained that these Mouk believers might not do it right, Mark assured them that they would be doing it in the same way he had done it and that it had to be this way because more doors were opening and he was unable to go to all the places himself. Therefore, the people in the village agreed to this plan.

By the time they went to the fourth village, the trained Mouk leaders did all the teaching while Mark watched. After that the Mouk leaders who were developing continued to go out to many other villages without Mark's direct involvement, starting new churches in each place. Over the course of time, some of them even began to go further away to villages they had had rivalries with, and out to people of other language groups.

This was a highly reproducible model for bringing the gospel to new places and starting new churches. It is, in fact, the model Jesus gave us! Our goal in developing "Share the Story" training has been to equip women and men in this kind of strategy using biblical storying because it is our passion to follow Jesus and fulfill his Great Commission to make disciples of all nations/people groups.

C. Foundational stories for a new church

As a new group of believers comes together and a church is established, strong foundations are important. So what sorts of stories can form these foundations for a new church?

Every church should make a long-range plan to bring all members through the Big Story, so they have a grasp of redemption history as it unfolds

> "Fast-tracking" is telling stories as a continuous series without pausing for dialogue or teaching, in order to preserve the developing storyline. In effect, it is stringing together several individual stories/episodes to form one narrative (i.e., the gospel). Some fast-tracks of the redemption story can be told in fifteen minutes or less. A prepared storyteller can expand the presentation by adding more stories and including more details and dialogue to fit the time and opportunity.

---

[8] Cross, J. R. (Writer and Director). *EE-TAOW!* (1999). Sanford, FL: New Tribes Mission.

through the Bible. In addition, it's important for Christians, especially new believers, to be equipped to share a "fast-tracked" version of the Big Salvation Story in one sitting.

In putting together a fast-tracked gospel presentation, we need to make sure we are clear on what the gospel is. Any gospel presentation must share the truth about how we all came to be separated from God due to sin (disobedience against him). Then it must include the truth that Jesus died for our sins, that he rose again to prove his claims that he is the Son of God, and that through him all people can be saved through repentance and faith.

Though it needs to contain the above components, this fast-tracked story will not be identical in every people group. For example, the good news for animists will include Jesus' power over the spirit world. Good news for Muslims includes Jesus' power to break us out of the futility of trying to gain salvation through our own efforts. Good news for Hindus will include Jesus' power to break the endless cycles and once and for all bring us into eternal relationship with God in a new heaven and earth. Good news for post-moderns includes Jesus' ability to truly change our lives and give us purpose and relationships that are eternal.

☞ How could you share in fifteen minutes the gospel story with the people you are trying to reach? In previous sessions you came up with a list of ten key stories that you could use to tell the Bible's Big Story of salvation. Drawing from that list and from what you know about your audience's culture/worldview, think about stringing some stories together to create a fast-tracked, fifteen-minute gospel presentation. (You may find it helpful to refer back to the discussion questions and activity at the end of Session 3, on worldview.)

Aside from the gospel, what other stories does a new church need to tell? As people hear the salvation story and come to faith in Jesus, they then need to know how to follow him. Stories from Jesus' life and ministry can help people learn how to be disciples.

Not only are stories of redemption history and discipleship important, but in a young church it is especially vital to tell the stories of how churches were started and how they multiplied in the book of Acts. Telling the stories of Acts chronologically reveals how a church came into being in Jerusalem after the day of Pentecost with the outpouring of the Holy Spirit, and how new churches were started throughout that region and right out to the ends of the known world in that generation.

D. Depending on the Holy Spirit

Sharing the stories of God's great salvation through Christ should lead us into an attitude of dependence on God's working among us and through us by his Holy Spirit. Our confidence is not ultimately in our strategy; our confidence must be in God, the promises of his Word, and his active presence among us.

As church planters, we must always be sensitive to the Holy Spirit's working in our own lives and in the lives of the people we have come to share the story with. This plan of action must remain flexible so we can respond to the Holy Spirit's activity among us.

☞ How can we model our dependence on the Holy Spirit to those we share the gospel story with?

It is Jesus who is building his church, and the gates of hell shall not prevail against it (Matthew 16:18). Followers of Jesus can expect to go everywhere in the power of the Holy Spirit and see people delivered from Satan's dark kingdom and made a part of Christ's glorious church. And we know this will happen time after time throughout all people groups until he comes back.

Questions for Discussion:

1. Do you think it is important to have a reproducible strategy (a vision for planting other churches) at the very beginning of starting a new church? Why/why not?

2. What reasons can you think of for using biblical storying as part of a church-planting strategy?

Activity:

The missionary Mark Zook used drama to communicate the Bible stories. In groups of two or three, choose a story and plan how your group could act it out. If you have time, maybe even have a quick practice and then act out your dramatic re-telling in front of the whole group!

SESSION 8: Where Do We Begin?

The following material is based on Video #8; if you have access to the videos, you can watch this session in advance, and then complete the study guide below.

Note: In this session, the "Activity" at the end will help you take the first step in putting all that you have learned into practice. If you haven't been able to do the Activities so far, we strongly recommend that you complete this sequence of Activities in Sessions 8-12.

I. Learner, Trader, and Storyteller

In 1984, my wife Marlene, our three children, and I traveled to Mexico to begin the process of learning the Spanish language and to set out on a new mission to share the good news about Jesus with the people of Latin America. Our question was, "But where do you begin?" Obviously, you must learn the language, but there is much more to it than that. You must become an insider within a culture that you did not grow up in. This appeared to me to be a daunting task, so I set myself to learn as much as I could. I read numerous books on the subject and spoke with many people I knew who had adopted a new culture.

I received much help from many sources, but one article by Donald Larson, a Christian anthropologist and linguist, proved to be of great help. It helped me avoid many of the pitfalls that new cross-cultural workers fall into. It also introduced me to biblical storytelling.[9]

A. Negative roles for those going to another culture

Larson shared that people in the indigenous culture tend to view a cross-cultural worker in one of three basic ways:
- as a teacher who has come to teach them something
- as a merchant who has come to sell them something
- as a judge who has come to accuse them of something

Getting placed in any one of these boxes can make it very difficult to become a true insider in your new adopted culture.

☞ Regardless of your actual job, why might being labeled and related to as a teacher, a merchant, or a judge hinder you in communicating the gospel to people?

B. Positive roles to seek

How can you avoid falling into these three categories? First, instead of seeing yourself as a teacher, you must enter your new culture as a "learner." Every person you encounter becomes your teacher. We discovered that even children love this teacher role as they tirelessly try to help you with language learning.

---

[9] Larson, D. (1978). "The Viable Missionary: Learner, Trader, Storyteller," *Missiology: An International Review, Volume 6 no 2*, pp. 155-163.

Secondly, you should gradually become a "trader" of life experiences with those in your new culture, rather than being understood as some sort of merchant or seller of ideas and religious materials. As we begin to share something of the story of our own life with others, they will naturally start to share something of their life with us. This helps create real relationships. Some of this trading can even be done without knowing much of the language.

> Some years ago we were in a small town in Ukraine where I was invited to speak at a church. After the preaching I was in the front praying with some people and noticed that a group of people had gathered around Marlene at the rear of the building. Later she shared with me what had happened. She always carried a small photo album with pictures of our children and grandchildren and representations of our lives back home. Since she only knew a few words of Russian, she began to show the pictures to some of the ladies there. Soon a small crowd gathered. One of the ladies left and then returned with a bottle of milk, giving it to Marlene and sharing that it was from their own cows. This was her way of "trading" life experience with Marlene, who had begun this interchange with pictures of our family. This was so human, so natural and so deeply moving. In that moment two lives were merging; friendship had begun.

☞ Can you think of a time in your own life when you were able to engage with someone as a "learner" of their culture or a "trader" of life experiences?

As language skills and understanding of the new culture develop, the third and most perilous box we must avoid is that of the "judge," the one who makes decisions on what must change in this culture. Instead of coming to point out all the things that need fixing, we must come as "storytellers." Once again this is the very stuff real relationships are made of. Friends tell each other stories. As we share our own stories as Christians, sooner or later we will tell stories about how we came into relationship with God through Christ.

II. Our Own Journey as Storytellers

All peoples have heritage stories-- stories of their history as a people. For those who know Jesus, many of the stories of our spiritual fathers are recorded in the Bible, and it is only natural for storytellers who follow Jesus to share these biblical stories they find most interesting and compelling.

As I was learning to speak Spanish, I began to work on some stories from the Bible so that I could share them with some degree of fluency. Finally I had about seven stories I could share in chronological order, beginning with the story of the creation of the world and ending with the death, burial, and resurrection of Jesus. I found joy in sharing these stories with friends and neighbors. I noticed, too, that they nearly always received these stories with interest, engaging in animated conversation. Often other family members or neighbors would join us when the time came to share another story.

We had rented a house from a man named Oscar, a well-known engineer who has spent most of his life in the city where we were working. When he asked what had brought us to Mexico, I shared with him about wanting to gather people and share the good news about Jesus that is found in the Bible. Not long after that Oscar came to me and said, "I would like to be your first student. I would like to know what the Bible says." I told him that it would be a great honor to begin to share stories from the Bible with him. We made a plan to meet one evening each week at his home. All his family members were invited.

On our first evening together I shared the story of God creating the universe. After I had told the story, we began to discuss it, and I asked, "What are some things you learn about God from this story?" Oscar quickly said that God must be incredibly powerful, very creative, and wise. The conversation went on to discuss how, if God created us in his own image, he must have done this so that we could have a relationship with Him.

At the end of our discussion time I shared briefly that God did indeed create us to have a relationship with him, and that even though the universe itself speaks to us about God, and our own consciences also indicate there must be a God, these things alone can't fully bring us into a relationship with him. God had to reveal himself, and he has done that through the Bible and through his only Son, Jesus, who came into this world to bring us into relationship with God. After I made this statement, Oscar said, "This is a miracle!" I thought the story and discussion time had gone well, but I hadn't thought of it as a miracle, so I asked what he meant.

Oscar said that it had been his habit for some time to get up early to pray. His prayer had been, "God, if you are there and you can hear me, please send me someone who will show me how I can know you." Then Oscar said, "I know God has answered my prayer tonight." There, at the dining room table, Oscar came to Jesus and received him as his Lord and Savior!

Oscar was a man of peace God sent to help us in starting that new church in Los Mochis, Mexico.

After that, sometimes we would even go out door-to-door and offer to share some stories from the Bible that would help people to understand the Big Story it tells. Within that informal context, we were sometimes surprised at how willing some of the folks were to hear the stories, and how they invited their friends over for the story sessions.

> J.O. Terry, in his book *Basic Bible Storying*, shares how many oral learners in particular are attracted to storytelling events. He says, "Because Bible Storying is an event, it is attractive and it fosters community, allowing a group to gather and participate. Group response reinforces the response of individuals in the group. One characteristic of oral learners is their preference to learn in groups vs. the typically individual learning of literates."[9]

My reason for beginning to tell stories from the Bible was initially based on a desire to function well within a new adopted culture. My experience showed that this approach opened doors and hearts. As we go to other people groups to share the good news about Jesus, we should be armed with a set of stories to tell, beginning with our own faith stories. This will lead to the stories from God's word that reveal to us who God is and who we are as his people.

---

[10] Terry, J. O. (2008). *Basic Bible Storying*. Fort Worth, TX: Church Starting Network. p. 10.

Questions for Discussion:

1. Can you think of a time when you shared your own story of coming to faith in Jesus and it led to further opportunities to share more stories about the Gospel?

2. What might your own tendency be -- to come to someone of another culture (or even your own) as a teacher, merchant, or judge? How can you fight these tendencies in yourself?

3. How do you think you would begin as a storyteller in a new culture?

Activity:

This Activity is the first in a sequence of Activities (in Sessions 8-12) that will help you practice the actual skills of storytelling and discussion-leading.

The first step is to choose a story from the Bible. This will be "your" story that you will work on memorizing, telling, and discussing over the next few sessions.

If there are just two or three of you completing this training, each of you should choose a separate story. If you are doing this training with a larger group, break into groups of two or three; each small group will choose a story to focus on.

Homework: Read and study the story that you (or you and your small group) have chosen.

SESSION 9: Preparing to Tell the Story, Part 1

The following material is based on Video #9; if you have access to the videos, you can watch this session in advance, and then complete the study guide below.

Note: In this session, the "Activity" at the end will help you put all that you have learned into practice. If you haven't been able to do the Activities so far, we recommend that you at least complete the sequence of Activities in Sessions 8-12.

Read the story of Jesus raising the paralytic, Mark 2:1-12.

I. Remembering the Story

It is vital that storytellers be very familiar with the story they plan to tell. Whether they tell it directly from Scripture or share it from memory in their own words, storytellers must maintain the expression and drama essential to a good story. It is certainly possible and sometimes necessary to read the story to the listeners, but there are great advantages to not being dependent on the text. Knowing the story well allows the freedom to tell it from memory at any moment.

Committing a story to memory does not actually require word-for-word memorization. As a matter of fact, trying to recite a memorized story is not always helpful since the mental exertion and fear of not getting it exactly right can cause you to sound stiff, and can communicate a sense of uneasiness to your listeners. It is usually better to simply tell the story in your own words while being faithful to the flow of the story as found in Scripture.

Let's take a look at some techniques you can use to help you remember stories from the Bible.

A. Use your ears and mouth

As you begin learning a story to tell, read it through out loud several times. Reading aloud gets the story "in" you through multiple channels: your eyes, mouth, and ears. Next, close your Bible and tell the story to yourself. After that, re-read the story to see if you forgot any important elements. Finally, re-tell the story, if possible to a friend, and as you do, try to picture the scenes of the story in your mind. Put yourself in the story.

I have found that what goes in through my ears comes more readily out of my mouth than what goes in through my eyes. I find it helpful to listen to the story being told on an audio recording. Many mobile phones have the capacity to record an mp3 file, so you can make your own recording to listen to. Then, after listening several times, you can practice telling the story.

B. Use headings

Nearly every story is made up of a sequence of short scenes or episodes. If we can remember the order of these episodes, it is easy to recall the flow of the story and tell it accurately in our own words. One way to remember this sequence is to give every scene a short title.

☞ In the story of Jesus healing the paralytic from Mark 2:1-12, what headings/scene titles would you use to help you remember the sequence of events? (Hint: I use ten headings. We've given the first one as an example. My complete list can be found on the last page of this session.)

1) In the town of Capernaum

Having this series of scene titles in mind allows you to easily tell the story in your own words without notes, yet also stay faithful to the Bible.

C. Use pictures

Another technique I use for remembering the story is to make stick figure drawings representing each of the scenes. This forms a little storyboard that reminds me of each episode. I have found this especially helpful in recalling the sequence of scenes in a long story. After you practice telling the story using the storyboard a few times, you will find that these pictures begin to stick in your mind, helping you to be note-free.

☞ Choose one of your headings from the question above. On a separate piece of paper, draw a symbol or stick figure scene that would help you remember that episode.

D. Memorize key phrases

In using these techniques for storytelling, it may be helpful to commit to memory the beginning and ending of the story, as well as particular phrases that are pivotal to the story.

☞ Look back at Mark 2:1-12. What sentence (or sentences) do you think is key, and therefore important to memorize word-for-word?

In the story of the healing of the paralytic, the sentence *"that you may know that the Son of Man has authority on earth to forgive sins, I say to you, rise, pick up your bed, and go home"* is very important in communicating the message of the story, so it's good to remember it word-for-word.

II. Telling the Story

Here are some practical guidelines for framing stories for maximum effect as you tell them.

A. The value of dialogue

When people speak within a story, they convey more than information: their dialogue delivers drama and reveals attitudes. Often in biblical stories, someone's heart is revealed by what they say or do rather than by a given description of that attitude (i.e., he was depressed, happy, or angry). Listeners, especially oral learners, tend to think of dialogue in real time and identify closely with the action, so a wise storyteller should capitalize on any dialogue in the story.

In some stories, information in the narrative can easily be changed into dialogue without altering the sense of the story. This can often be a good option in framing the story for telling.

Read Matthew 2:1-7.

This story already contains a lot of dialogue, but there are a few places where you could turn some of the narration into dialogue. What extra sentences of dialogue could you add if you were telling this story?

In written form, a person's quotation may be broken in two with a reference in the middle, telling us who is speaking: *"Look," said John the Baptist, "the Lamb of God."* In storytelling, however, it is helpful to tell who is doing the talking beforehand and then follow with an uninterrupted dialogue quote: *John the Baptist said, "Look, the Lamb of God."* Also, clearly stating the speaker's name often through the dialogue helps the listeners follow who is talking to whom.

As you clarify who is talking to whom, you may find it helpful to consider a formulaic name for particular characters involved in the drama. For example, when referring to God in a story, it can be confusing to switch from "God" to "Lord" to "Father." People who are not familiar with all these terms for God in the Bible may find this hard to follow.

To build consistency in the stories we have prepared to share among the Ndebele-speaking people in Africa, we have used "Creator God" as the name for God, especially throughout the first stories in the Old Testament. As we move chronologically through the stories, we begin to introduce other names for God, such as "Lord God" and "Father." In another example of formulaic names, I recently told the story of Balaam and Balak in Africa. Because these names can be confusing, I used the formulaic names, "King Balak" and "Soothsayer Balaam" for these two main characters in the drama.

B. Non-verbal communication

When using dialogue in the story, some dramatization is effective. Verbal dialogue and non-verbal communication go hand in hand.

What kinds of non-verbal communication can you think of?

When telling the story of the healing of the paralytic, I will often *locate* myself off to the side as I depict the religious leaders talking among themselves, assuming a hunched over *stance* with *hand gestures* and *side glances* that depict deep concern and confusion. When Jesus replies to them, knowing what their questions are about, I return to the middle of the area, stand upright and speak with a *tone* of sincerity and gentleness back toward the area I have established for the religious leaders huddled together. At this critical moment in the drama of this story, after Jesus' essential commentary to them that he does indeed have the power to forgive sins on earth, I *pause*, slowly *turn* toward the paralytic who is lying directly in front of Jesus and say to him with an exuberant *tone* that comes when you know something wonderful is about to happen, "Get up! Take your mat and go home!" And the man does get up! All eyes are now on Jesus; he is the hero of the story.

As you can see from this example, the storyteller's location, posture, gestures, movement, pauses, and tone all help bring the story to life for the listeners. Eye contact with the listeners may also have a strong effect at certain moments in the drama. (This is highly variable from culture to culture. In some cultures it is not considered appropriate to make eye contact with those being spoken to. You should learn the storytelling norms of the culture you are in.)

Let's focus more closely on tone of voice. Regardless of which sections of dialogue we choose to include in our story, the way we deliver that dialogue can make a big difference to our listeners' understanding of the story. The storyteller, though being faithful to the text, begins to actually interpret the text as he or she speaks-- and tone of voice is a key part of that interpretation. Think, for example, of the different tones in which Pontius Pilate could say to Jesus, "What is truth?" (John 18:38) Depending on how you interpret his character (from clues in the rest of the story), you may give him a genuinely questioning tone, or you may make him sound cynical and wary, asking a rhetorical rather than a genuine question.

A good storyteller must also be able to identify the way the listeners will relate to the story's drama, and adapt his or her tone accordingly. When I tell the story of Jesus healing the paralytic, I am careful about my characterization of the religious leaders. As I share the response of the religious leaders to Jesus' forgiving the paralytic of all his sins ("Why does he say these things? This is blasphemy! Only God can forgive sin!"), I am careful not to use a cynical tone because I am conscious that some of the listeners probably have this same question in their minds; they identify with the religious leaders. I express their questioning as genuine concern and confusion on their part as they struggle with what Jesus has just said. In this way, I make sure that I'm not alienating my listeners. Then, when I come to Jesus' reply to them, I try to use a tone of voice that is kind rather than accusatory. In this way, the hearers realize that Jesus genuinely desires the religious leaders to know who he is, and he also desires the same for the listeners themselves.

C. Preserve the flow and suspense of the story

Expositional teaching often involves language that distances the speaker from the material being discussed. Phrases like, "Many would say that," "We see in the text," "Scholars tell us that," "There are three possible interpretations of" are commonly used. This kind of commentary does not make good storytelling. Such "distance language" usually introduces a variety of ideas that are hard to remember and that detract from the drama of the story. Good storytellers do not feel they must explain every tension the story produces; rather, as they tell the story, they allow the suspense to build and questions to arise. Suspense and conflict build interest; commentary undermines good drama. Opportunity to discuss any issues and questions the story has provoked in the listeners will come in the discussion after the story.

Sometimes you may think it essential to explain something in order for the story to make sense. You can give any necessary historical/cultural/biblical context in your introduction to the story, or save it for the discussion at the end. It's best not to insert explanatory notes during the story, unless they are very brief. For example, you might say, "Naomi replied, 'Don't call me Naomi [which means pleasant]. Call me Mara [which means bitter] because God has dealt very bitterly with me'" (Ruth 1:20).

Jesus was a master of using the tensions and questions a story could produce. Think of the parable of the weeds sown into the field, and how his listeners might have mentally reacted as they heard it (Matthew 13:24-30):

> Jesus says, "Here's what the kingdom of heaven is like. It's like the owner of a field sowing good seed into his field."
> *Listeners think: O.K. Just as I suspected -- God's heavenly kingdom is purring along nicely.*
> "But later, in the night while everyone is asleep, his enemy sneaks into the field and sows weeds among the wheat. Then he leaves."
> *Hang on. Who is this enemy? What's he doing in this story?*
> "When the wheat sprouts and grows, the weeds pop up too. The farm hands say, 'What's going on? You sowed good seed into this field; what are all these weeds doing here?'"
> *Now there's a good question. Maybe we'll get some answers now.*
> "The owner answers, 'An enemy has done this.'"
> *Yeah, we already know that, but what's he doing in this story? This sounds a little too much like our own story now.*
> "The farm hands say, 'All right then, do you want us to start pulling up these weeds?'"
> *Right on! Let's deal with this problem right now and get it over with.*
> "The owner answers, 'No!'"
> *No! What do you mean "No"?*
> 'You might uproot the wheat along with the weeds. Let them grow together. When harvest time comes I will tell the harvesters to bundle up all the weeds for the fire; then they will gather the wheat into my barn.'"
> *Now that has a serious ring to it. How is this supposed to apply to my life?*

The story is so intriguing, so unsettling, so close to home, that the hearers are left hoping for another story shedding more light on the subject. As a result the door remains open, even among the listeners who aren't at all sure they want to believe what they are hearing. At the same time, those who genuinely want to understand more about the kingdom of heaven receive further light and understanding as they interact and dialogue with Jesus. (Jesus explains the meaning of the parable in Matthew 13:36-43.)

Questions for Discussion:

1. How did Jesus tend to deal with the questions and tensions his stories produced?

2. In groups of two or three, read John 4:1-26 aloud. Have one person read the dialogue for Jesus, and the other person read the dialogue for the Samaritan woman (if you have a third person, he or she can be the narrator). After you've read the story, talk about the different tones of voice you could use for the woman when she says "I have no husband." What tone of voice do you think Jesus would have used when he replied? Share your ideas with the larger group.

Activity:

This Activity is the second in a sequence of Activities (in Sessions 8-12) that will help you practice the actual skills of storytelling and discussion-leading. Last session you chose a story from the Bible that will be "your" story.

Homework: Use some or all of the techniques you learned from this session to help you remember your chosen story. Practice telling your story aloud. It is your choice whether to sit or stand as you tell the story. As you practice, think about the following: explaining any context you might need beforehand, highlighting key dialogue within the story, and using location, posture, gestures, movement, pauses, and tone of voice to make the story come alive.

Next session, you will practice telling your story to your small group of two or three.

Note from Part I, section B: When telling the story of Jesus healing the paralytic from Mark 2:1-12, I will have in my mind the following scene titles.

1) In the town of Capernaum
2) Jesus teaching in a crowded house
3) Four friends bring a paralytic
4) Up on the roof
5) Inside the house
6) "Your sins are forgiven"
7) Religious leaders say to each other "How can he say this?"
8) Jesus says to religious leaders "Why do you think these things?"
9) Jesus says to the paralytic "Get up, pick up your mat and go home!"
10) All the people say, "Wow, we have never seen anything like this!"

SESSION 10: Preparing to Tell the Story, Part 2

The following material is based on Video #10; if you have access to the videos, you can watch this session in advance, and then complete the study guide below.

Note: This session, the "Activity" at the end will help you put all that you have learned into practice. If you haven't been able to do the Activities so far, we recommend that you at least complete the sequence of Activities in Sessions 8-12.

I. More Tips for Telling the Story

In the last session, we began to examine some techniques to bring Bible stories to life for your listeners. Here we add a few more "tools" for you to consider as you prepare your stories.

A. Give attention to word usage

As I have already mentioned, dialogue between characters in the story adds life and a personal touch to the story. However, dialogue can slow the story down a bit. Verbs, on the other hand, tend to move the action along at a better clip.

Whenever possible, think about using vivid verbs. In the story of Jesus healing the paralytic (Mark 2:1-12), for example, the text says, "They *removed* the roof above him, and when they had *made an opening*, they let down the bed on which the paralytic lay" (verse 4b). This translation is fine, but the Greek verbs used to describe their action can carry a more aggressive, violent feel. The verb "remove" could be translated "unroofed," and "made an opening" carries the thought of "breaking it up." So when I tell this story I usually say something like, "They *tore* up the roof and *broke* a hole through it." I accompany this sentence with physical actions that suggest tearing through the tile roof with some destructive force (see Luke 5:19). I believe this is true to the actual account, and at the same time it adds compelling action to the story.

Just as verbs move the action of the story along, adjectives and adverbs give the story color and feeling. For example, in the story of the baptism of Jesus, the Father speaks from heaven and says, "This is my beloved Son, with whom I am well pleased." The adjective "beloved" adds emotion and affection to the word "Son." Also, "well" is an adverb that adds strength to "pleased."

As you can see, giving careful attention to the details of the story is an essential part of effective storytelling. As we seek to maintain the discipline of not embellishing the story to the degree that it loses its actual flow and meaning as it stands in Scripture, we can also choose words of action and color to bring the story to life.

B. Vocal variables to consider

As we discussed last session, varying tone, pitch and volume with our voices all make for more effective storytelling. Simply our tone of voice and the pace of our words can convey a wide range of emotions and attitudes. Depending on tone and volume, a single phrase can carry a feeling of either grief or pain or a bold statement of fact.

For example, as I tell the story of the woman at the well from John 4, when Jesus asks the woman to go and get her husband, she answers, "I have no husband." As I picture this lady who has had five different husbands and now lives with a man whom she is not married to, my decision is to let her answer be full of emotional pain, not a bold declaration. So as I speak her words I do not say them in a bold declarative manner; rather, I avert my eyes away from Jesus, looking to one side, downward, saying slowly, struggling with every word, almost in a whisper: "I-- have-- no--h...husband." When I say the words "no husband," it is almost as though I'm spitting them out in agony. When I then give Jesus' reply, "You are right when you say you have no husband," I make sure there is no tone of accusation in his words, just the fact he clearly knows her story and is about to bring salvation and healing to her broken life.

I know that choosing to use these tones for the woman and Jesus is interpretive. A storyteller must do interpretive things without apology. That is our job. It is important that we are so familiar with God's Big Salvation Story that we do our interpretation in the light of the whole story.

Pauses in storytelling are also effective. Pausing can add emphasis to what you have just said. When I am telling the story of Adam and Eve in the Garden of Eden from Genesis 2, and I come to God's warning not to eat of the tree of the knowledge of good and evil ("When you eat from this tree, you will certainly die") I slow down for that phrase and then pause. This casts a very sobering atmosphere over the statement. Picking up the story again, we go right into a wonderful love story of Adam and Eve happily married and running naked together through the Garden. But that one highlighted phrase will be key for the listeners to remember in the next story (the disobedience of Adam and Eve in Genesis 3).

Often beginner storytellers are nervous, so they rush through the story too quickly. Planning a few significant pauses in the story can help you remember to slow down. Also, the practice of pausing can be very useful if you forget momentarily what comes next in the story! A short pause and a deep breath are often all you need to do in order to recall what follows.

C. Develop good beginnings and endings

A good storyteller gives special attention to how a story begins and how it ends. A good beginning draws listeners in from the start. Many biblical stories start with a brief look at the larger surroundings and then very quickly zero in on the main character or characters of the story. The story of the healing of the paralytic begins with a brief glimpse of the town of Capernaum and the fact that Jesus has returned from a ministry trip and is now home once again. Then the story zooms in on the action that is happening at the house where Jesus is staying and the great crowd that has gathered there. The story pulls us right into the center of the action. It is important to take special note of the way biblical stories begin, and to learn to capture that drama in the storytelling.

The ending of the story is equally important. The end of the healing of the paralytic story is loaded with excitement and amazement. As the paralytic is on his feet leaving the house with his bed under his arm, the story winds up like this: "Everyone was completely amazed and began praising God, saying, 'Wow, we have never, ever seen anything like this before!'" Now that's a good ending.

Many Bible stories end with a surprisingly brief and punchy statement. It is important to maximize such endings. Often, I have noticed the group wants the story to carry on, and they are left reflecting on the story, trying to assimilate what they have just heard. That is a vulnerable moment and we storytellers must allow this to happen.

It is very helpful for the listeners to understand when the story has started and when it has finished. Virtually every culture has ways of signaling when a story has started. For many of us, to hear the phrase "Once upon a time" signals that a story is about to be told. The same story may well end with, "And they lived happily ever after." These phrases indicate for most of us that the story being told is fictional. Therefore, this <u>would not</u> be a good way to start and finish a true story from the Bible. Most cultures have ways to indicate that a true or heritage story is coming. We could signal a true story by beginning the story within a recognizable historical context and ending it in the same way.

Usually when starting a biblical story I will say something like, "Now I want to tell you a story from the Bible," and finish with, "That is the story I wanted to tell you from God's word." These cues let the listeners know when the actual Bible story has begun and ended, distinguishing it from the storyteller's explanatory preface or "teaser" for the next story (see below). I will often finish by stating the chapters where the story is found and encourage people to read the story for themselves. This is also an encouragement for them to bring their Bibles so that they can refer to the story during discussion times in future storytelling sessions.

After finishing the story, whenever possible, you can open up a time for questions and discussion (we will talk about how to facilitate that in Session 11).

D. Link chronological stories

When telling biblical stories chronologically, part of thinking about your story's beginning and ending is to provide links between the previous story, the current story, and the upcoming story. These links show the stories' continuity and triggers listeners' recollection of previous stories.

How do you link stories? Before you launch into your story for the day, tell a short bridge story, connecting the present story with the last story. After you finish your story, you can include a "teaser" or preview to create anticipation for the next story. Serial stories, young adult chapter books, and soap operas have used this technique with great success for years. Just a short statement like, "You're not going to believe what happened next" or "In our next episode we are going to tell you about the time when [then add a provocative statement about what's coming]."

II. General Principles for Paraphrasing

Many storytellers wonder how closely they should stick to the text when telling a story from the Bible.

A. Light Paraphrasing

I have generally recommended "light paraphrasing." This means that you do not try to tell the story from rote memorization, but rather, tell it in your own words after becoming very familiar with it, closely adhering to the way it is given in Scripture.

As biblical storytellers, we must give attention to telling the stories with accuracy and faithfulness to the text. At the same time, there should be a sense of freedom to tell the story in our own words, in a way that communicates to our audience. There will always be a tension between these two factors since good storytelling requires some artistic skill and dramatic presentation--but these creative elements must be subject to Scripture.

Light paraphrasing is especially helpful when you want to summarize extended stories (for example, the life of Abraham) or craft composite stories from different parts of the Bible (for example, the creation of the spirit world). You can also use this method to bring a particular focus to aspects in the story that have particular relevance for your group.

B. Deep Paraphrasing

Some speakers preach in a narrative way that often goes further than this light paraphrasing. They do "deep paraphrasing" by adding color and details to the story that are not actually found in the Scripture. Usually this kind of deep paraphrasing has to do with the particular purpose or agenda of the speaker who is preaching the sermon. This approach serves best when the hearers are already familiar with the actual story in the Bible or have just read that story at the beginning of the sermon. I would not recommend this type of deep paraphrasing when sharing with those who are depending on you for the actual story from the Bible. If they are oral learners or those without knowledge of the stories from the Bible, it is important to stay true to the content of the story in Scripture without interjecting lots of our own flourishes and commentary.

When it is necessary to inform the listeners of background information that might help them correctly understand the story being told, it is better to tell that background story or share that information before you begin telling the story. Too much explanation during a storytelling session can undercut the power and drama that the story itself brings.

C. Verbatim

Finally, let me say that there is a time and place for a verbatim telling or reading of the story. In certain cultural contexts it would be very appropriate to memorize a story word for word and tell it accordingly, or to give a dramatic reading of the story directly from the Bible. For example, some Muslims would feel that a verbatim reading is how all sacred text should be communicated. This method places a strong emphasis on accuracy to the Bible and shows our high value for Scripture.

One disadvantage of this method is that sometimes the story contains extra detail (names, places, numbers) that do not translate well into the oral context, and that compete for attention with the main purpose for which you are telling the story. Another disadvantage is that a verbatim telling/reading would make it more difficult to tell both a summary of a long story and a composite of several stories.

Based on the context they are in, biblical storytellers must make these kinds of decisions regarding the amount of liberty they will take with the text.

Questions for Discussion:

If you are not able to discuss these questions with a group, completing them in written form on your own will provide you with a way of engaging with the material from this session.

1. Each one of the short stories below contains dialogue between characters. In groups of two or three, select one story and think about the emotions that were likely connected to the words the characters were saying. How would those words sound in your voice when you tell that story? Practice the dialogue out loud, experimenting with different tones of voice.
   - Genesis 22:5-8 (Abraham and Isaac)
   - Genesis 50:15-21 (Joseph promises to provide for his brothers)
   - 2 Samuel 9:1-8 (David shows kindness to Mephibosheth)
   - Daniel 3:13-26 (Shadrach, Meshach, and Abednego)
   - Mark 7:24-30 (Jesus and the Syrophoenician woman)

2. In the story your group has selected from above, choose one or two places where you think a pause would be appropriate for emphasis.

3. How would you tell the beginning and ending of this story? Think about the following:
   - linking to a previous story
   - giving any needed context/explanation for this story
   - using a cue phrase to signal that the story has started
   - how you would tell the actual start of the story itself
   - how you would tell the end the story itself
   - using a cue phrase to signal that the story is finished
   - linking to the next story by giving a "teaser"

Activity:

This Activity is the third in a sequence of Activities (in Sessions 8-12) that will help you practice the actual skills of storytelling and discussion-leading. So far, you have chosen your story, memorized it, and begun to practice telling it using various dramatic techniques.

For this session, tell the story to the other member(s) of your small group. As you listen to each other, give each other suggestions on how to improve the telling of the story. Remember to comment on things like:
   - Beginning and ending (including context, beginning/end cues, linking stories)
   - Use of dialogue
   - Pace and pauses
   - Non-verbal techniques (location, posture, gestures, movement, tone of voice)
   - Word choice (verbs, adjective, adverbs)

Homework: Use the feedback that your group members gave you and practice telling your story a few more times. Try to make it as good as you can! Next session, you will work on formulating discussion questions for your story.

SESSION 11: Helping People Engage with the Story

The following material is based on Video #11; if you have access to the videos, you can watch this session in advance, and then complete the study guide below.

Note: This session, the "Activity" at the end will help you put all that you have learned into practice. If you haven't been able to do the Activities so far, we recommend that you at least complete the sequence of Activities in Sessions 8-12.

I. Benefits of Group Discussion

After the storyteller has shared the story from God's word, it's important that people have a chance to internalize the story. A small group discussion is a wonderful context for this kind of engagement.

Discussion allows the listeners to begin to discover truth for themselves as they think and talk about it together. In this context of discovery, a deep and abiding kind of learning takes place. If all our teaching is simply giving out predigested material, our hearers may never learn to grapple with and digest the truth of God's word for themselves. I believe this is a main reason why God gave us stories of real people in real places encountering the reality of God in their lives. He gave us a book of stories that comprise the Big Story rather than giving us a point-by-point theological textbook. Through discussing these stories, people gain tools to think through and apply God's truth for themselves.

Those of us who are teachers are often tempted to try to explain everything as we share a story from God's word. We deeply want to solve every unanswered question that may arise as a result of the story. However, this tendency can unintentionally undermine the opportunities for growing together that can happen as the group begins to dialogue and deal with questions the story provokes.

☞ What are some of the benefits of having a small group context for hearing and responding to these Bible stories?

You may be able to think of many advantages of small group discussion. Here are a few that I've found important.

A. Remembering the story

First of all, small group discussion helps each group member to remember the story. It's hard to forget a story that you have personally discussed and wrestled with in terms of its meaning and relevance. I have found that often when people discuss a story they are much more apt to want to go to their Bibles and delve further into it later on. This is a good reason for telling the group where the story is found in their Bibles.

> I remember storytelling in a village where many, especially older people, did not know how to read. After telling the story I told them where the story was found in the Bible so that they could read it for themselves later. There was an elderly grandmother there who could not read; she quickly told her young literate grandson next to her, "Write down where the story is in the Bible so you can read it again to me later!"

It can also be helpful to retell or reconstruct the story in the next session before moving on to the subsequent story. Doing this can help the group remember the previous story and build a bridge to the next story when they are being shared in chronological order. The leader can ask the group to think back to the last story, and group members can take turns retelling short segments of the story with different people chipping in until the whole story is told. The group leader may need to ask questions to keep the group moving, such as, "And what happened after that?" or "Does anyone remember what happened next?"

This reconstruction is best done in a lighthearted atmosphere. Usually when someone makes a mistake or can't remember the details, the group will self-correct. However, if it becomes clear that the story has not been really understood or remembered, the leader can take the opportunity to retell the story again before moving on. Retelling the story can also provoke further questions or discussion around that story, and serve as a way to follow up on the application points the group arrived at in the previous session.

For an example of how to reconstruct a story as a group, you can watch the beginning of Video #13.

B. Building relationships

Another advantage of discussion after listening to a story is that it helps relationships grow in the group. In this process of discovery together, we begin to engage in one another's lives. People will naturally begin to share life issues that somehow connect with the story. This open sharing allows us to begin to truly be a community of people on a journey together.

People may also share personal needs, which give us opportunity to go to God together in prayer regarding that need. Significant encouragement and healing can happen in this context.

> I was once telling the story of how God created Adam and Eve in the beautiful garden he had prepared for them, and how he had joined them together in marriage. We were in a culture where polygamy is a fairly common practice. As we discussed the story as a group, we observed how marriage was God's idea, and it was the joining of one man and one woman in a "one flesh" relationship. A lady present in the group asked this question: "I'm one of four wives. How am I to relate to this story?" Needless to say, everyone in the group was all ears. In the discussion that followed words were shared that may have helped this lady, but what happened to me was that I found myself praying for her throughout the week, asking the Lord to help her walk with him and receive encouragement from him as she faced this difficult situation. The next time we met as a group I could not help but rejoice when I saw her there, ready to hear another story from God's word.

C. Revealing spiritual progress and understanding

Discussion can also help inform those who lead the group where the various members are in their journey with the Lord. We talked earlier about the need to recognize where our group members are at in their growth toward maturity as disciples of Jesus (Session 6).

Listening to people's questions and responses to the story can also alert us to misunderstandings about the story. This insight can help the storyteller lead the discussion further by asking more questions that can help clear up the misunderstanding. If the misunderstanding is a result of an opposing worldview issue, then this may help the storyteller select other stories that will continue to address that particular cultural stronghold.

D. Communicating openness

Discussions around the stories also communicate to the group that it is okay to have questions and doubts. We must trust that the Holy Spirit can work through these stories. They are transformative. They are relevant to life in any place or period of history. We do not have to defend them; our part is simply to tell them. When Jesus told stories, he allowed people to walk away with questions in their minds; however, it seems that very often they came back again to hear another story, because they had been provoked by the previous story. An open, caring, supportive small group will help those on the edge of faith to keep coming back.

II. Questions to Facilitate Group Discussion

What kinds of questions will help people engage with the story through discussion? For some discussion leaders who are just beginning, structured questions can be helpful in order to make sure that the group covers the main issues in the story. Leaders with a bit more experience can get the ball rolling with some basic questions which may naturally trigger further questions. *(For another helpful framework for discussion, see Appendix E: Leading Discussion with Head-Heart-Hand Questions)*

A. Start with open-ended questions

Begin with some simple questions about the story just to build the group members' confidence to participate. A question like, "What caught your attention in this story and why?" can be helpful. Another open-ended question could be, "What questions do you have about the story?" There are no right or wrong answers to these questions, but discussion has begun. You could also ask questions about the story's content ("What happened when...?"). These questions can serve as a review of what the group has heard.

B. Focus on God

As discussion begins to move forward, I like to ask, "What did you learn about God from this story?" Or if it is a story about Jesus, "What did you learn about Jesus?" This kind of question is a constant reminder that the triune God is not only the author of these stories, but he is also their primary character.

C. Think about the characters

Then I like to ask, "What did you learn about the people in this story?" This question helps us discover the attitudes and motives of the people who are involved. This question may allow the group to face some of their own issues at least in an indirect way. These discussion times should make people feel safe to share their own story with the group.

D. Apply the story

Finally, it is good to finish by asking, "What will you take home from this story?" or "What have you learned from this story?" or "Is God telling you anything about your own life through this story?" The response to these application questions may be personal or group-wide. You can encourage people to think about their response in a community context by asking something like, "What action could we take as a group to live out this story in our neighborhood?" As discussion facilitators, we should encourage individuals and the group as a whole to begin to enter and "live" the story.

While we were in Zimbabwe during a time of great economic crisis in the country, we went to a small group that was doing Chronological Bible Storying. The previous week they had heard and discussed the story of Abraham and how he believed God. As we were beginning, the group leader asked if anyone had anything to share that God had done in his or her life over the last week. One lady told this story:

> During the week we completely ran out of food at our house. I had enough money to buy a sack of maize meal, but not enough to ride the bus to town. I asked around if anyone was planning to drive into town and no one was. It was then that I remembered the story of Abraham and how he believed God. I decided that I would follow in his steps and believe God. So I set out walking towards town [about a 10 mile walk], not knowing how I would be able to walk the distance back home carrying a large sack of maize meal.
>
> As I walked along, I looked down and there at my feet was some money-- enough to get on the bus and travel into town, buy the maize meal, and return on the bus back home and have some money to spare! God met me and provided for me just as he had done for Abraham.

That lady had entered the story and experienced God's wonderful provision. After that we were all challenged in our hearts to take greater steps of faith in our walk with God.

E. Other useful discussion-leading tips

- Give people time to think and respond. Rephrase the question if no one is answering.
- Affirm people's responses; when appropriate, reflect their responses back to them ("So, what you're saying is...?")
- If someone shares something, ask follow-up questions to help the group go deeper.
- Reel people in from tangents by saying something like, "Let's come back to the story..."
- Encourage quieter people. You could say, "Let's give opportunity for some who have not shared anything yet to say something."
- Avoid giving your own opinion too much-- this will shut down discussion.

III. Developing a Safe Atmosphere

☞ Think about any small groups you have been part of. Have you been part of a group that felt like a safe community? If so, what made it feel that way? If not, why not?

Often at the beginning of a storytelling session I will share the following basic ground rules which help us maintain an environment where we feel safe to open up our lives to each other.

- First, we want to allow for transparency as we share. There are no questions or doubts that are out of bounds. Each member of the group must feel free to share from his or her heart, without fear of reprisal or debate.

- As we open up and share what is in our hearts, we will not make it our job to try to "fix" each other. We will not try to be therapeutic; we will not turn our times together into counseling sessions. If a need is shared, then at some point we may ask if the person would desire to receive prayer regarding the matter. It is God who is able to heal and restore us.

- Thirdly, we will endeavor to use "I statements." Instead of saying "everybody says" or "the church says," I will try to share what I think. I will endeavor to tell you what is actually going on in my own heart and mind.

- Finally, we will try to avoid "cross talk." This is what we do sometimes when we feel someone is struggling to say something, so we try to help out by putting words in their mouth for them. Or it's what can happen when someone is sharing something that is difficult or emotional to share, and we try to lighten the atmosphere by saying something funny. These dynamics do not help create a safe place to open up our lives together around God's Big Salvation Story.

In maintaining a safe atmosphere where all can feel liberty to share what is truly happening in their lives, we have found that in most cases it is best if the children are taken out during the discussion time. Someone from the group could lead an activity and/or a time of discussion about the story that is especially appropriate for their age. (However, we usually encourage children to stay with the adults and listen to the story before going out, since even from a young age children can hear and relate to stories!)

IV. Using the Bible Text During Discussion

Based on your group and culture, you may choose to use the actual Bible text in different ways during discussion.

1. After the story has been told, rely on the group's memory of the story and use the storyteller as a resource to help recall the details of the story during discussion. This is helpful for guests to feel that they are on an equal footing with everyone else in terms of their ability to contribute to the conversation. This method also serves oral learners. It works well for long, extended narratives and for composite stories that do not refer to just one Bible passage.

2. If you want to focus on accuracy to the text (for example if you are giving a verbatim telling or reading of the story), you can bring Bibles and announce the page number, or print out copies of the Bible passage for everyone. This way, the group can refer to the text while they listen to the story and discuss. This eliminates confusion from using different translations and ensures that all group members, including guests, are (literally) on the same page. This method is helpful if you have a group who do not all share the same native language; seeing the words as well as hearing the story can help them follow along. This method would not be good for cultures where there are significant numbers of oral learners, and it would not work so well for long summaries or composite stories.

3. People bring their own Bibles and can refer to them while they listen to the story and discuss. The pros and cons of this method are similar to those listed in #2 above. Do be aware that being called

upon to lookup passages in the Bible can be off-putting for guests or new Christians who either don't have Bibles or don't know how to find the passage in the Bible. The leader can also announce where the story is found in the Bible so that people can look up the passage on their own later.

I would encourage people to bring their Bibles to any biblical storytelling session when possible. It is good for them to be able to refer to the story being told and discussed as it is written down in the Scriptures. Sometimes I will ask the group after I have shared a story, 'did I forget any important part of the story?' This sort of interaction reminds the group the final authority regarding what these stories say is the Bible itself. I would not generally encourage in a Storying session a lot of technical discussion over words and phrases. That might be a valid part of a class on biblical hermeneutics but will likely cause guests and those who have no biblical background to feel at a disadvantage and unable to enter into the discussion. The very best discussion times generally are people sharing their own responses, questions and stories without a lot of time on technical 'Head' discussion and never getting to the 'Heart' and 'Hands' (*see Appendix E: Leading Discussion with Head-Heart-Hand Questions*).

Questions for Discussion:

1. Can you think of a time when you entered into the life of a story from the Bible in your walk with God?

2. How would you go about building a sense of community and safety within a new biblical storying group?

3. What are some advantages you see in having discussion around the story that has been told?

Activity:

This Activity is the fourth in a sequence of Activities (in Sessions 8-12) that will help you practice the actual skills of storytelling and discussion-leading. So far, you have chosen your story, memorized it, and practiced telling it using various dramatic techniques. This session, you will think about leading a discussion on it.

For this session, the Activity is different depending on whether you are doing it with just a pair/threesome, or whether you have a large enough group to have split into several sets of pairs/threesomes.

If there are only 2 or 3 of you: Each person has chosen his or her own story to tell. Take some time as individuals to think of questions you could use to draw out the most important points in your story. In the final session, each person will be telling his or her story and leading a short discussion on it.

If there are several sets of 2/3's: In your small group of two or three, you are sharing the same story. Talk about your story together and come up with questions you could use to draw out the most important points in your story. In preparation for the final session, divide the story and/or questions between you; as a small group, you will be telling the story and leading a short discussion on it for the larger group as a whole.

Homework: If you have access to the videos, watch Video #13, a model story-telling and discussion session of the story of Noah. (You could also review Video #12, the story of Cain and Abel.) This will help you "put all the pieces together" as you prepare for your final activity: leading a storying session on the story you have chosen.

SESSION 12: Practical Activity

> *If you have access to the videos, you will find it helpful to watch Video #13 first, a model storytelling and discussion session of the story of the Flood. This will help you solidify all that you have learned about storying. This session also provides an example of how to help the group "reconstruct" the previous story, helping the listeners better remember it.*

Congratulations! We've arrived at the final session of this Share the Story training track. It is important to do the practical application in this session. These last four sessions have helped you practice the actual skills of storytelling and discussion-leading. So far, you have chosen your story, memorized it, practiced telling it using various dramatic techniques, and decided what questions you will ask for discussion. As the culmination of the "Share the Story" course, you will now have the chance to tell the story and lead discussion on it in a small group.

This session will be structured differently depending on whether you are doing the course with just a pair/threesome, or whether you have a large enough group to have split into several sets of pairs/threesomes.

If there are only 2 or 3 of you: All of you should take a turn to lead your own storytelling/discussion session. You should tell the story you have been working on, and then lead a ten to fifteen minute time of discussion about it. The other members of the group should then give you constructive feedback on both your storytelling and discussion-leading.

If there are several sets of 2/3's: Each small group takes a turn to lead a storytelling/discussion session. All the group members should be involved in some way, either telling the story or leading the time of discussion about it. Also, consider having someone in your group lead the listeners in a reconstruction of the story after the story is told. This reconstruction of the story should be light-hearted and enjoyable for everyone. This can be a valuable way of helping those hearing the story to remember the story told.

After the storytelling session with discussion, the other groups should then give them constructive feedback on both their storytelling and discussion-leading. The amount of time you spend on each story will be determined by the number of groups you have; you may need to spread the storytelling/discussions over a couple of sessions. Taking the time to practice what you have learned is an essential part of development in this strategy. On-going times practicing with others your storytelling and discussion-leading skills is of real value as you continue on this journey of Biblical Storying.

Through this course of training we have learned the importance of sharing the story of the gospel with those who have not yet heard the good news. We have learned the cross-cultural value of being a biblical storyteller. We have considered the important part Biblical Storying plays in making disciples and starting new churches. We have begun practicing the techniques of good storytelling and discussion-leading.

My prayer for you is now that you have completed the "Share the Story" course, you would find many opportunities to put what you have learned into practice in many creative ways in your life as a follower of Jesus. May you be ready to share God's Story in one-to-one discipleship and evangelism, in small groups, or in a whole church setting.

Thank you so much for taking time to do this training. May God's richest blessing be upon you as you continue to tell the greatest story ever to fall upon human ears.

We would love hear how your journey into Biblical Storying is going. Please feel free to contact us at info@biblicalstorying.com and share your experiences, stories and questions with us.

Appendix A:
Orality and Literacy Worldwide

Many people would think of oral learners as those who are illiterate. It is certainly true that those who cannot read are oral learners. But many people in the world have technically learned to read, yet reading is not their primary means of learning.

We often assume that everyone who has learned to read will be able to learn effectively through primarily literate means. Many missiologists are discovering that this is far from being the case-- and that orality is much more prevalent than literacy as a means of learning. Dictionaries define orality as "a reliance on spoken, rather than written, language for communication."

One of the problems we face is that most statistical reports on the world's literacy are proving to be unreliable. In 2011 the United Nations Educational, Scientific, and Cultural Organization (UNESCO) reported that 83.7% of adults and 89.3% of youth worldwide are literate. This became a widely accepted statistic even though UNESCO added a disclaimer stating that the data is not reliable because it is usually based upon the individual's self-declaration of their literacy or on the completion of a certain number of years of schooling. They went on to say that the more reliable means of understanding people's literacy ability is to assess them directly in surveys that actually test their skills.

The National Adult Literacy Survey (NALS) did this more in-depth testing in the 1990s in the USA. It was found that 48-51% of adults in the U.S. scored at the two lowest literacy levels (out of five levels). Similar results emerged in Australia, Belgium, Canada, Denmark, Germany, Ireland, Portugal, Poland, New Zealand, Switzerland, the United Kingdom, and elsewhere. Most of these people could read a little bit and would have been counted as literates, but would not have been able to do the full range of tasks in order to function as a literate person in those societies.

It would be safe to say that these people (about half the population) would function in reality primarily as oral learners. These more developed nations count for about one sixth of the world's population. The other five-sixths would tend to have much lower functional literacy rates. Therefore, the estimate that two-thirds of the world's population are oral learners is a very conservative one.

In light of this massive prevalence of orality, as followers of Jesus we must take into strong consideration how oral learners best learn. We must begin to incorporate oral communication strategies effectively as we seek to carry out Jesus' commission to us.[11]

---

[11] Much of the information in this addendum is from an article by Grant Lovejoy, (2012). "The Extent of Orality: 2012 Update." International Missions Board. Retrieved from https://orality.imb.org/files/1/1255/Lovejoy--Extent%20of%20Orality%202012.pdf

Appendix B:
The Value of Biblical Storying in Post-Modern Culture

The Rise and Fall of Modernism

Since the Age of Enlightenment beginning in the 17th century, the rationalistic/scientific approach to truly knowing anything became the centerpiece of Western culture. With this cultural development came a huge optimism that the scientific method would solve the greatest problems we face in the world. Many people believed that human reason alone would lead us to objective truth and answer our fundamental questions about life.

This worldview (Modernism) gave rise to single, rationalistic explanatory systems that tried to account for all the main issues of life. Some of these explanatory systems have been called socialism, communism, capitalism, fascism, etc.

After World War II, these rationalistic explanatory systems came under severe criticism by some Western European philosophers, largely because they saw the terrible results of fascism in Hitler's Germany and the Marxism-Leninism in Stalin's Soviet Union. They began to refer to these systems of thought as "totalizing stories" or "meta-narratives" that allowed people to act in brutal ways toward others who did not agree with them. These philosophers felt the only answer was to "deconstruct" and do away with all of these meta-narratives that had caused people and nations to feel they had the right to global power and the right to force others to submit to their system. This thinking began to be referred to as "post-modernism."

Distinctives of Post-Modernism (A Cultural Shift)

One of the effects on culture that post-modern thought has produced is a deep distrust of all "totalitarian" explanations of the world we live in. Therefore, individuals and groups should be free to create their own worldviews. Their personal stories become their interpretive framework; their own experiences become the basis for their knowledge.

Because of this encouragement of multiple worldviews, post-modernism idealizes pluralism and tolerance, especially with regard to matters of faith or religion: people with divergent views are to be given a hearing and allowed a place among all the other stories being told. Post-modernists, however, would be pessimistic that they could find any objective truth in this process. Realms of knowledge should be "probed" rather than "proven."

This attempt to do away with the existing meta-narratives soon has begun to give way to new meta-narratives flying under the banner of words like "development" and "social justice."

Barriers to the Gospel within Western Culture

There may be particular biblical accounts that cause real questions and concerns among those who fear narratives that give people a sense of entitlement to exercise force or violence toward other people. An example of this might be the story of the Lord God calling the Israelites to go out against the city of Jericho and completely destroy it (Joshua 6). It is important that we see how Jesus brought a transition, from the physical warfare in these Old Testament stories about the Israelites, to the spiritual warfare now to be fought by his followers.

For example, as Jesus was being arrested in the Garden of Gethsemane, the apostle Peter grabbed his sword and was ready to battle the mob (he did manage to chop off one man's ear!), but Jesus told him, "No more of this! Put your sword back in its place. For those who take the sword will perish by the sword." Then Jesus promptly healed the man's ear (Matthew 26:52, Luke 22:49-5, John 18:10-11). This and many other stories of Jesus make clear that such physical warfare and violence done in Jesus' name, to promote his mission on the earth, are not legitimate in any way for us as his followers. We are not called, nor are we able, to enforce his story through our own power. The big story of the Bible, which finds its center in Jesus, will lead us to the attitude described by the apostle Paul when he said, "our struggle is not against flesh and blood, but against...the spiritual forces of evil in the heavenly realms" (Ephesians 6:12).

Bridges for the Gospel within Western Culture

For followers of Jesus who desire to share the new life he brings to those influenced by present post-modern Western culture, there is some good news. As we have seen, Post-modernism values individuals' stories, and each of us has a story to tell of how trusting in Jesus has changed our lives. We also have heritage stories to tell of others who have encountered God's salvation through trusting Jesus. The Bible contains many such stories.

One of the great advantages to Biblical Storying, especially in today's Western culture, is that it encourages open dialogue around the story being told. The very nature of sharing the stories of the Bible requires a kind of humility not found in those who believe they are the enforcers of a "totalizing story" or "meta-narrative." We must listen to the views of those who hear our story without being critical or rejecting toward them. Jesus himself often responded to questions from his hearers with another question. This approach can be the best way to respond to some people because it can lead them to a process of discovering truth, in a way that a straight-on argument rarely does.

We must realize that willingness to engage in this sort of dialogue does not diminish our witness for Christ, but can extend and deepen it. After all, any true dialogue presupposes commitment to a view on both sides. Therefore, as Christians we must feel the freedom and conviction to share the good news about Jesus with those around us. At the same time, we must hold our view in humility and vulnerability because we are not able to make God's story of salvation happen; it is not possible for us by our own power or ability to bring people to faith in Jesus. Only God can bring his story to its proper conclusion in history and in people's hearts. Lesslie Newbigin put it succinctly with these words: "if the biblical story is true, the kind of certainty proper to a human being will be one which rests on the fidelity of God, not upon the human knower. It will be a kind of certainty which is inseparable from gratitude and trust."[12]

---

[12] Newbigin, L. (1995). *Proper Confidence*. Grand Rapids, MI: Eerdmans. p. 28.

Biblical storying's humble, dialogue-friendly approach actually stems from the Bible itself. The gospel message is not given to us as a set of abstract statements to simply be declared to others. The Bible is primarily made up of particular stories from different times in history about real people encountering God in a variety of cultures and situations. All these stories are brought into clear focus and fulfillment through the story of Jesus coming into the world and his death, burial, resurrection and ascension. This very character of the biblical story gives it its unchanging nature as the story of God's salvation for every nation. But there is a highly relational component to the way the gospel comes to us, which quite naturally should include two-way conversation between people. This has been a real part of the gospel story truly being shared with those who have not yet heard in every generation and culture. This must certainly be true of those of us who seek to share this story in Western culture.

As we share the story, God's great salvation message has its own power because the Holy Spirit works through it. After all, he is the only one who can change hearts and bring people to real faith in Jesus. Telling the stories of the Bible is an effective way of sharing the good news about Jesus among people of every nation and culture, including people in Western culture. We must pray that the Holy Spirit will do his work among those who hear.

Appendix C:
The Story of Redemption

Below is a list of key stories that we developed for use in Zimbabwe. Depending on cultural context, this can serve as a basic list in telling the great Salvation Story of the Bible. Audio versions of these stories can be found on the website, biblicalstorying.com, under the Resources tab (login required).

1. Creation of the world (God is all powerful and all that he does is GOOD)
2. Creation of man and woman (God's plan and purpose for mankind and his design for marriage)
3. Creation of the spirit world (needed in Zimbabwe due to fear of the spirit realm and dead ancestors; may be optional in other cultural situations)
4. The first sin and judgment (here's where all of our trouble begins)
5. Cain and Abel (God knows what is in people's hearts and takes note of what they do)
6. Noah and the flood (God is not distant; he takes an active role in judgment and salvation)
7. The Tower of Babel (all man-centered attempts to reach heaven will fail)
8. God's promise to Abraham (called to bless all peoples)
9. Abraham and Isaac (God provides a substitute sacrifice)
10. Joseph (How God used Abraham's descendants to bless the nations)
11. The Passover (because of the blood of the lamb, God's judgment passes over the Israelites)
12. God gives His holy law (the Ten Commandments given to the Israelites)
13. The sacrificial system (shedding of blood to cover sins so God could dwell among his people)
14. Story of David (the great deliverer-king)
15. The prophets' message of a coming redeemer/king who would suffer for the sins of mankind
16. Birth of Jesus according to prophecy (Jesus' birth was the fulfillment of God's promises)
17. Baptism of Jesus (this story includes each person of the Trinity)
18. Jesus and Nicodemus (the new birth)
19. The paralyzed man and four friends (Jesus has power to forgive sin)
20. The parable of the prodigal sons and the compassionate Father
21. Healing the blind man (Jesus has authority over sickness and disease)
22. Calming the sea (Jesus has authority over nature)
23. Gadarene demoniac healed (Jesus has authority over demons)
24. Lazarus raised from the dead (Jesus has authority over death; he is the resurrection)
25. The parable of Abraham, Lazarus, and the rich man (we must believe the message of the Scriptures for salvation; a dead man was not allowed to come back for that purpose)
26. The last supper (Jesus fulfills all the Passover lamb points toward)
27. Jesus' betrayal, arrest, and trial (Jesus is the perfect and spotless Passover Lamb)
28. The crucifixion ("It is finished!" Jesus completes the work he has come to do)
29. The resurrection & appearances to disciples and followers (Jesus literally, physically rose from death)
30. The ascension (Jesus gives his disciples final instructions and returns to the Father in heaven)
31. Pentecost (the outpouring of the Holy Spirit and Peter's message to the crowd)
32. Jesus, the High Priest (Jesus alone is our Great High Priest and Mediator between God and us; ancestral spirits cannot do this)
33. John's vision of Jesus' second coming, his final judgment, and his reign in the new heavens and new earth (this story is helpful in Zimbabwe to show the final judgment for all evil, including evil spirits, and the final triumph of Christ with his people forever. May be optional in other cultural situations)

Appendix D:
Exercise in Story Selection
with a Focus on Worldview Issues

When we were beginning to prepare our first set of stories in Zimbabwe, we formulated a set of questions to ask the native people, questions which addressed their worldview issues. These included

- Where did the world come from?
- Where did the first people come from?
- What is the most important thing in your life?
- Where do you go when you die?
- Are there good spirits or evil spirits?
- Where do these spirits come from?
- Who rules over these spirits?
- Who decides what is wrong or right for a person?
- What happens when someone does wrong? Is there any punishment? By whom?
- How important are traditions to you here among your people?
- Are the traditions you grew up with being passed down to the next generation?
- What role does work play in your life?

The following statements are based on interviews with people of rural Zimbabwe in answer to various worldview questions.

Regarding the spirit world:

A supreme being made the world. He made mankind too. This supreme being or force is distant, and communicates via the spirits.

The spirits are good and evil. When we die, we enter into this spirit world. It is the same place where our ancestors are, wherever that is. The spirits of our dead ancestors carry messages between the supreme god and the living people. The supreme god made the world and he made us, but he is far away; we can only communicate with him via the spirits.

We are very concerned about the attitudes of the spirits of our dead because they are the ones who can take direct action on our lives. We brew ceremonial beer, offer sacrifices, and other such acts to appease the spirits in order to keep peace in the family and in our lives. When they are not appeased they may cause lack of employment, infertility, sickness, unrest in the family between husbands and wives, and even death.

How one lives has little effect on where one goes, but can affect the type of spirit which lingers in the family of the living. This is how a family can have a history of theft or hard work: the dead person lingers in the form of a spirit and affects those still living. These spirits can influence every part of life.

We have much respect and fear of the "traditional healers" (*nyangas*) and mediums because they can contact and communicate with the spirits of the ancestors. They are able to discover the specific ways to remove curses and misfortune.

Regarding what is right and wrong:

Family and community are the most important things to us. Respect and good standing are important in our community, and help us maintain good behavior and do what is right.

Our community determines what is wrong or right. Our elders in the community, such as the chief and headmen, determine what a punishment will be by considering the severity of the crime. Due to this we feel it is very important to honor the leaders in our community. It is very important to be thought well of in the community. Spiritually, the supreme god works through the ancestral spirits to bring down judgment on wrongdoing.

There is only a limited amount of "good" in the world. The person who has much good coming to him has it at the expense of someone or something else. Too much ambition for the good can be dangerous and cause suspicion in the community. He may be trying to work magic to get the good.

Regarding work:

Work is an activity no one can escape. I do not enjoy work very much; it is a necessary evil.

Regarding the importance of traditions:

Our traditions are very important. When someone leaves to go overseas they are still encouraged to practice the traditions we have. Our traditions are usually passed down to the head of the family. They tell all the family the stories about the traditions again and again. They lead in doing the traditional things in all appropriate situations.

Also, songs are sung at ceremonies and beer brewings that speak of the traditions. Chiefs and elders play a key role in such events in the community. These influential people often remind us of how these things should be done at public meetings (funerals, weddings, etc.).

Those of us who are not people of position are afraid that if we discuss details of these traditions with outsiders, the spirits may not be happy with that.

Things were better in the old days when the traditions were held up more strongly.

Activity

Break into groups of two or three. As a group, look for any barriers and bridges to the gospel in the statements these rural Zimbabweans made. Next, choose ten stories from the Bible you feel would help address the barriers and connect with the bridges. Finally, share your list of stories with the whole group.

Appendix E:
Leading Discussion with Head-Heart-Hand Questions

In their book, 'Truth That Sticks', Avery Willis Jr. and Mark Snowden suggest thinking of questions in terms of "the head," "the heart," and "the hands" as a guide for effective discussion around the story that has been told[13].

Head questions deal with the content of the story. It is important to make sure that the hearers of the story have captured what the story actually says. Questions that deal with the content of the story such as, "Can you remember the names of the main characters in the story?" or "Where does the story take place?" You may ask about key things that happened in the story. If it comes clear that significant parts of the story were misunderstood a retelling of the story might be in order. Also questions about how they responded to the story can be helpful. For example, "What caught your attention in the story?" or "What are some of the problems or difficulties presented in this story?" or "What about this story caused questions to arise in your mind?" Responses to these types of questions can help alert the discussion leader to any misconceptions or worldview barriers that might be present among the hearers.

Next, we go on to some **heart questions**. These questions deal with the implications of the story and lead us toward the discovery of insights that come to us through the story. For example, I often begin with a question like, "What did you learn about God from this story?" and then continue with, "What did you learn about the human characters in this story?" We may go on to ask about the insights that people are receiving from the story. It is important to make these questions open-ended, questions that cannot be answered with a simple "yes" or "no." During this time, some people may want to share a story from their own life that the story brings to mind. This can prove to be a vital aspect of the discussion time. If the responses begin to stray away from the primary focus of the story it can be helpful to refocus the group back onto what the story itself says.

Finally, we come to the **hand questions**. These are application questions; they call for action. To start this part of the discussion I may ask, "What do we need to take home with us from this story?" or "What do you believe God may be saying to you through this story?" The story may be calling for repentance in some area or steps of faith we need to take. This may well lead into ministry time in the small group where the gifts of the Holy Spirit are used to strengthen and bless various members as they seek to respond to the Lord. The result may bring different responses in different individuals in the group. Alternatively, being informed by the story the whole group may take action together to reach out to bless their neighborhood or friends who have not yet come to faith in Jesus or in some specific ways commit to prayer for particular people or needs represented in the group.

Activity
Break up into groups of two to four. Give each group a story from one of the gospels. After reading the story together, discuss the primary reason you would want to tell this story in your small group.
Next, develop a list of head, heart, and hand questions you could ask that would help serve the people in your small group in responding to truth(s) the story leads us to. Share these with the larger group.

---

[13] Willis, A. T. and Snowden, M. (2010). Chapter 5 in *Truth That Sticks*. Colorado Springs, CO: NavPress.

Appendix F:
Selected Recommended Reading

For further understanding of the strategy of Biblical Storying

Basic Bible Storying: Preparing and Presenting Bible Stories for Evangelism, Discipleship, Training, and Ministry by J.O. Terry. Fort Worth, TX: Church Starting Network, 2008.

> Terry brings decades of experience as a pioneer of Biblical Storying into this book. He puts special emphasis on the vital importance of adapting this strategy so that it is particularly suited for a new target group. He says, "Bible Storying is for everyone and can be adapted for teaching all who will listen. This manual guides those who embark on the journey to realize how to do this task."

Truth That Sticks: How to Communicate Velcro Truth in a Teflon World by Avery T. Willis Jr. & Mark Snowden. Colorado Springs, CO: NavPress, 2010.

> Willis and Snowden bring a strong focus on the value of Biblical Storying in the United States (and other Western cultures). This book also very helpfully focuses on the value of Biblical Storying as a means of developing a disciple-making church. They give clear instruction for utilizing this strategy particularly in small groups that are both relational and purposeful in sharing and living the message of the gospel.

Telling God's Stories with Power: Biblical Storytelling in Oral Cultures by Paul F. Koehler. Pasadena, CA: William Carey Library, 2010.

> Koehler has served for many years endeavoring to communicate the gospel message in parts of the world where people are unaccustomed to a Western style of learning. This book focuses a great deal on the reality of the world of orality and how oral communicators differ in many ways from that of print learners. This book will be of great help especially to those who desire to use Biblical Storying in cross-cultural contexts.

For training in the art of biblical storytelling

The Art of Storytelling: Easy Steps to Presenting an Unforgettable Story by John Walsh. Chicago, IL: Moody Publishers, 2014.

> Walsh gives important tools for effective communication of stories. This book contains helpful exercises in storytelling that would facilitate a group seeking to improve their skills, whether they are beginners or those already experienced.

Story Journey: An Invitation to the Gospel as Storytelling by Thomas E. Boomershine. Nashville, TN: Abingdon Press, 1988.

>Boomershine uses the gospel of Mark as a basis for illustrations of biblical storytelling. He shows the importance of giving attention to the details of the story and studying the text in order to be a faithful biblical storyteller. He says, "We need to recover the Gospel as storytelling. Story is the primary language of experience…Through the stories Jesus becomes present."

Printed in Poland
by Amazon Fulfillment
Poland Sp. z o.o., Wrocław